CAMBRIDGE LIBRARY COLLECTION
Books of enduring scholarly value

History

The books reissued in this series include accounts of historical events and movements by eye-witnesses and contemporaries, as well as landmark studies that assembled significant source materials or developed new historiographical methods. The series includes work in social, political and military history on a wide range of periods and regions, giving modern scholars ready access to influential publications of the past.

Brief Notices of Hayti

John Candler (1787–1869), a Quaker Abolitionist, visited the West Indies between 1839 and 1841, to study the situation of ex-slaves since they had obtained their freedom. He spent three months in Haiti, and appears to have been generally impressed by what he found. The former slaves had become smallholders, growing crops on small plots of land, though they were not interested in producing more than they needed for their basic livelihood. The export of coffee, cotton and tobacco had declined since the end of slavery, and the sugar trade had ended. Whites were barred from owning land, or from marrying Haitians, and were restricted in trading activities, reducing available investment capital. The compensation demanded by France to the former plantation owners was also crippling the economic development of the island. Candler's book gives much valuable detail about an important former colony at a time of transition.

T0382510

Cambridge University Press has long been a pioneer in the reissuing of out-of-print titles from its own backlist, producing digital reprints of books that are still sought after by scholars and students but could not be reprinted economically using traditional technology. The Cambridge Library Collection extends this activity to a wider range of books which are still of importance to researchers and professionals, either for the source material they contain, or as landmarks in the history of their academic discipline.

Drawing from the world-renowned collections in the Cambridge University Library, and guided by the advice of experts in each subject area, Cambridge University Press is using state-of-the-art scanning machines in its own Printing House to capture the content of each book selected for inclusion. The files are processed to give a consistently clear, crisp image, and the books finished to the high quality standard for which the Press is recognised around the world. The latest print-on-demand technology ensures that the books will remain available indefinitely, and that orders for single or multiple copies can quickly be supplied.

The Cambridge Library Collection will bring back to life books of enduring scholarly value (including out-of-copyright works originally issued by other publishers) across a wide range of disciplines in the humanities and social sciences and in science and technology.

Brief Notices of Hayti

With its Condition, Resources, and Prospects

JOHN CANDLER

CAMBRIDGE
UNIVERSITY PRESS

CAMBRIDGE UNIVERSITY PRESS

Cambridge, New York, Melbourne, Madrid, Cape Town, Singapore,
São Paolo, Delhi, Dubai, Tokyo, Mexico City

Published in the United States of America by Cambridge University Press, New York

www.cambridge.org
Information on this title: www.cambridge.org/9781108024389

© in this compilation Cambridge University Press 2010

This edition first published 1842
This digitally printed version 2010

ISBN 978-1-108-02438-9 Paperback

BRIEF NOTICES

OF

HAYTI:

WITH ITS

CONDITION, RESOURCES, AND PROSPECTS.

BY

JOHN CANDLER.

LONDON:

THOMAS WARD & CO., 27, PATERNOSTER ROW;

AND

CHARLES GILPIN, 5, BISHOPSGATE STREET WITHOUT.

1842.

INTRODUCTION.

In bringing before the public a view of the present
state of Hayti, it seemed desirable to prefix to the
narrative, a brief sketch of the history of the island.
The Author had intended to prepare such a sketch;
but upon examining those works, both French and
English, which are considered as authorities, he
found so many discrepancies and counter statements, involving the character of several of the
leaders in the late revolution, that he abandoned
the attempt in despair. The history of Hayti has
yet to be written, nor can it be written impartially,
so as to establish the truth, and the whole truth,
till the present generation shall have passed away.
The literary public of France and England may
yet look for an accession of historical materials,
that will throw great light on the late contests
between the free and the servile classes, and between
the whites and the men of colour. The present
Secretary of State for Hayti, General Inginac, who
is now advanced in age, and who was engaged in
the wars of the revolution, almost from his boy-
hood, has prepared a narrative of the passing events
of the period, both civil and military, which is
intended for publication at his decease. This nar-

rative, when published, will, no doubt, illustrate
many circumstances that are now obscure, and
serve to unfold more clearly the character and
motives of some remarkable men, his contemporaries. It is the delight of the lovers of liberty to
dwell with enthusiasm on the talents and exploits
of *Toussaint L'Ouverture*, undoubtedly the greatest
man that took part in the revolution of St.
Domingo, and one of the ablest Generals of his
age; but it is very doubtful whether his character,
as a leader in the great struggle, will come out
of the crucible of impartial history, with all that
brightness and purity that some modern narratives,
half history, half romance, seem to assign to it.
The opinion of many persons in Hayti, whether
well or ill-founded, we stop not to inquire, is certainly adverse to such high pretensions: these
individuals represent *Toussaint* as one of the best
men of his day; but not as free from many of
the blemishes which generally attach to warriors.
The lines of Pope are become an axiom, and are
often quoted as decisive with regard to men who
are engaged in the dismal work of slaughtering
their fellows:

> " All heroes are alike : the points agreed ;
> From Macedonia's madman to the Swede."

and it is remarkable to observe, as a confirmation
of the poet's doctrine, which is true to a certain
extent, that the character of Hannibal, as penned

by the severe and vigorous hand of Juvenal,
has been accommodated by Dr. Johnson in his
" Vanity of Human Wishes," to represent the
life and exploits of Charles the Twelfth ; and that
the portrait drawn of the latter, might, with the
omission of a line or two, and the change of half a
dozen words, be made literally to apply to Napoleon
Buonaparte. If there be any exception to the truth
of Pope's apothegm in modern days, that exception
may undoubtedly be made in favour of *Washington*
and *Toussaint*. But those great men who act in
a public contest, where the passions of a whole
people are stirred up and roused into revengeful
activity, however mild they may be by nature, and
however disposed to act with mercy, often contract
the stains that attach to the party they embrace,
or the cause in which they embark, and exhibit in
their conduct more than a common frailty. The
civil wars of Hayti are now ended ; and happy
would it be for humanity's sake, if we could draw
the curtain of night on the many dark transactions
that disgraced the period of their progress ! The
people of that country, however, have learned from
them an awful lesson ; and this one good consequence has resulted, that the Republic, weary of
contending with the sword, is now desirous of
keeping it sheathed in the scabbard, and of maintaining an honourable and lasting peace.

The author of the following " brief notices"
declines the task of an historian ; but if his pages,

which are intended to exhibit the present state of Hayti, with its resources and prospects, should afford amusement or instruction, in any degree, to those who read them, his end will be fully answered, and he will receive all the reward he desires or looks for.

York, Third Month, 1842.

CONTENTS.

HAYTI.

CHAPTER I.

THE island of Hayti, formerly Hispaniola or St.
Domingo, placed between the 18th and 20th degrees of
north latitude, and from 68 to 75 degrees west, has a
length of 360 miles from east to west, and a breadth,
varying from 60 to 120 miles. Its circumference measured by an even line, excluding the bays, is nearly
a thousand miles. This island so important for its
situation and great natural advantages, is four times
as large as Jamaica, and nearly equal in extent to
Ireland. It is situated at the entrance of the Gulf
of Mexico : is one of the four larger Antilles, and holds
the second rank after Cuba, from which it is distant
only twenty leagues. Jamaica lies westward of it
about forty leagues; and Porto Rico, a large and now
populous island belonging to Spain, twenty-two leagues
eastward. On the north are the Bahama islands, at a
distance of two or three days' sail ; and southward,
separated by 700 miles of ocean, is the great continent
of South America.

B

The principal islands adjacent to Hayti and belonging to it, are Gonave, La Saone, Isle de Vaches, and Tortue, all of considerable extent ; but all through the policy of the government uncultivated. Hayti presents the aspect of a large territory composed of mountains and plains, watered by a few extensive unnavigable rivers and innumerable streams : it abounds in forests of mahogany wood and other fine timber—affords a great variety of climate ; and, displays a grandeur and beauty of natural scenery, not surpassed in the tropical regions of the New World, or perhaps of the globe itself.

Like all the other islands of this region, it is subject to awful tempests, known by their Indian name of hurricanes, and is liable to frequent shocks of earthquake. The latter formidable phenomenon in 1564, destroyed the newly founded city of Concepcion de la Vega, and has occasioned at several different and distant periods, the overthrow or disturbance of Port au Prince, its present capital. A line of demarcation, in some places artificially drawn, formerly separated the Spanish part of the island from the French ; but there is now no political distinction of territory, the whole country being united under one political head subject to the same laws. The ancient part of the island where the Spanish language is still spoken, embraces more than two-thirds of the soil, and contains only one-sixth of the inhabitants. The population of the Spanish part is estimated at a hundred and thirty thousand ; of the French part, nearly seven hundred thousand. The French or western territory, is the only part of the island that has numerous towns and villages, and it is here principally, that commerce carries on its exchanges with other nations. A large quantity of mahogany

wood is exported from Santa Domingo, and a good deal
of tobacco from Santiago and Port au Platte, all towns
once belonging to the Spaniards, and still Spanish as to
language and the customs of the people; but the great
staples of coffee, cotton, mahogany, and dye-wood, are
collected on the French side and shipped from Cape
Haytien, Port au Prince, Cayes, Gonaives and Jacmel.

The mountains of Hayti are many of them of great
height. The principal range, is that of Cibao, near the
centre of the island, from which other chains of hills
diverge in different directions. The peak of Cibao is
7200 feet above the level of the sea. The mountains
bearing the name of La Selle, Le Mexique, and Le
Maniel, are parts of the same range terminating on the
southern coast. La Selle has an elevation of 7000 feet,
and bears south-west of Port au Prince, at a distance of
forty miles. The La Hotte mountains rise in the
neighbourhood of Cayes, some of which are said to be
as high as those of La Selle and Cibao. Besides these,
there are the mountains of Monte Christo running from
the north of the island eastward to the Peninsula of
Samana, from the summits of which, Columbus gazed
with astonishment at the extent and fertility of the
plains below, since that period deprived by death and
massacre of its original inhabitants, and now known by
the expressive name of *la despoblada* or the unpeopled.
The other ranges are those of Cahos and Los Muertos,
which are rather hills than high mountains, having a
mean elevation of about 2500 feet. " This configura-
tion," says Moreau de St. Mery, " and the height of
the mountains is the cause why, notwithstanding the
great extent of many of its plains, the island when
viewed from seaboard appears mountainous altogether,

and that its aspect is so forbidding. But the observer," he continues, " who contemplates these vast chains and all the branches that diverge from them, and pursues their various ramifications over the surface of the island, will see at once the cause of its fertility : they form an immense reservoir for the waters which are distributed to the soil by rivers without number: they temper the heat of a burning sun, arrest the fury of the winds, and multiply the resources of human industry to an astonishing extent."

The most spacious of the plains, is that of Vega Real, which traverses several of the northern departments : its length is 220 miles: it is exceedingly fertile and well watered. Its chief produce, is tobacco of an excellent quality : it grows also sugar and cocoa, and affords pasturage to large herds of cattle ; but owing to its present sparse population, yields comparatively little of food or agreeable luxuries to the wants of man. The noble rivers Yague and Youna which traverse its whole extent, will serve greatly to facilitate the transit of its produce, whenever a large and active body of settlers may devote themselves to the cultivation of its soil. This plain alone might well support its million of inhabitants. That of Santa Domingo is the next in importance, and has very few people upon it, although from its fertility and extent of surface—700 square leagues— it would yield, if cultivated, an immensity of produce. The plain of Azua has a surface of 150 square leagues, and that of Neybé eighty square leagues. Of the remaining plains, it is only needful to mention, La plaine du Nord, near Cape Haytien, and Le cul de sac, near Port au Prince, in both of which, sugar was formerly cultivated to a great extent, and

where a large number of sugar works and distilleries
are still in operation to furnish syrup and rum for the
home market.

The principal rivers are the Yague and Youna before
mentioned and the Artibonite, whose entire course is
160 miles long in almost a direct line, and which, during the time of its floods, floats on its bosom to the sea,
those vast logs of mahogany that find so ready a sale in
the markets of Europe, under the name of Spanish
mahogany.

Hayti has some lakes of considerable size, where
alligators abound : it is rich also in mineral springs, and
is believed to possess vast treasures of iron and copper
ores, together with gold and silver. The mines that
contain the precious metals have long since been abandoned for want of capital.

Such in its physical structure, is one of the islands
we proposed to visit on our leaving home in 1839, for
a voyage to the West Indies.

CHAPTER II.

In the latter part of the year 1839, I left home,
accompanied by my wife, on a missionary tour to
Jamaica. After stopping by the way at Barbados,
Martinique, Tortola, St. Thomas, and Porto Rico, our
vessel the Hecla steamer made for the windward
passage, and coasted the northern shores of Hayti.
The bold outlines of the mountains, which in many
places approached to within twenty miles of the shore,
and the numerous stupendous cliffs which beetled over
it, casting their shadows to a great distance on the
deep—the dark retreating bays, particularly that of
Samana, and extensive plains opening inland between
the lofty cloud covered hills, or running for uncounted
leagues by the sea side, covered with trees and bushes,
but affording no glimpse of a human habitation—presented a picture of gloom and grandeur, calculated
deeply to depress the mind; such a picture as dense
solitude unenlivened by a single trace of civilization,
is ever apt to produce. Where, we inquired of ourselves, are the people of the country? Where its cultivation? Are the ancient Indian possessors of the soil
all extinct, and their cruel conquerors and successors
entombed with them in a common grave? For hundreds of miles as we swept along its shores, we saw

no living thing, but now and then a mariner in a solitary skiff, or birds of the land and ocean sailing in the air, as if to shew us that nature had not wholly lost its animation, and sunk into the sleep of death. Towards the north-west extremity of the island our course became a little enlivened : we entered the bay of Cape Haytien, formerly Cape François, since Cape Henry, and now, for brevity's sake, The Cape. The terrible fortress of La Ferriere, which commemorates the rule of Christophe, and which serves as a mausoleum for his remains, looked down upon us from a distant mountain; two forts commanded the entrance to the harbour, in which were numerous merchant vessels lying at anchor, taking in or discharging their cargoes ; and on our right hand, flanked by forest-crowned hills, rose the city itself, once denominated the little Paris—the handsome city of the queen of the Antilles. Our stay was short: we landed for two hours, left the mail from Europe, spoke to the British Vice-Consul, visited the markets, conversed with a few of the black citizens, and again set sail. Before we had passed through the narrow strait that separates Tortue (the Turtle island) from the main-land, we were gratified with a distant view of the town of Port de Paix, rising in amphitheatre on the hills, illumined by the rays of the setting sun. Soon after we headed the Cape St. Nicholas Mole; and the following day landed at Santiago, the eastern capital of Cuba. Here as at Cape Haytien our stay was limited to the time allowed for post-office business ; the next day we reached Kingston in Jamaica. It is not the object of this little volume to detail the incidents of our travels in Jamaica, an island so often visited and so well known ; but we cannot, in connexion with it, avoid a brief notice of that memorable event which has done so much to change the condition of ·its people, and seems fraught with such inestimable blessings to posterity. Here we trace the interesting spectacle of a colony, once deeply distressed and clamouring for fiscal aid to the mother-country; now smiling in prosperity and brightened by mercantile hope; not long since distracted by civil disturbances, the fruits of oppression inseparable from its institutions; now enjoying peace and tranquillity, with a docile, loyal, industrious population, whom the Queen of England, or the ruler of any nation, might well be gratified to own as subjects. The grand experiment of giving unqualified freedom to the slaves of Jamaica and our other West Indian islands, has been attended with the happiest success. All classes of the population rejoice in the result. The prognostications of the planters and the mortgagees of colonial property, that the slaves when emancipated would become an idle vagabond race, a nuisance to the soil—that the fields would go out of cultivation—the lives of the white inhabitants be endangered—and the properties ruined—these and other prophecies of the same sackcloth cast, are all falsified by the most gratifying facts. Just the reverse of all this has taken place; and Jamaica and the other islands have begun a new race of prosperity. "*Magnus ab integro sœclorum nascitur ordo.*" The labourers work well for wages, and squatting and vagabondage are unknown. The cane and coffee fields partially neglected at the coming in of freedom, owing to the injudicious attempts of overseers and attorneys to coerce labour, by means of rent, are recovering their former fruitfulness. Two years have passed away in which we have seen diminished produce, the consequence of unwise conduct on the part of the planters; and a third, in which the deficiency has sprung from a visitation of Divine providence in a long continued drought. Sounder views of political economy, and a wiser conduct than was once pursued have succeeded; the seasons are again propitious, and there is now every reason, with regard to the future, to look for extended commerce and increased prosperity. In passing through Jamaica (and we went into almost every district) we scarcely met with a single individual who seemed to regret the change that had taken place—not one who professed a wish, even for gain's sake, to return to the former system of slavery. We conversed with men of every rank and condition, from the Governor and Judges of the island to the Clerk who serves in the counting-house, and all bore their unqualified testimony to the important fact, that freedom works well. That it works well for the labourer is obvious at every step of the stranger's progress: the proofs are on every hand; that it works well for the proprietor is demonstrable by a few simple and striking facts. The estates of proprietors, in numerous instances, are worked at a less cost now than under slavery. Penn or pasture land, we were told as a matter of common observation, may be worked cheaper than before: some of the large coffee plantations we know are so worked, from the testimony of the managers themselves; and we have in our possession a letter from the attorney of some of the largest sugar estates in the island, in which he distinctly tells us, that he sees no reason why sugar properties in the district where he lives should not be cultivated as cheap as ever they were. To all the proprietors of such lands,

it is quite evident, that the share of the twenty millions
which fell to their lot, was given them for nothing.
The compensation money paid by Great Britain to the
planters, however it might be intended to operate, serves,
not as an indemnity to meet losses accruing from the
great and happy change from slavery to freedom, but to
clear off the accumulated and fast increasing incum-
brances which the oppressive and wasteful system of
slavery had induced. A large proportion of the estates
in the West Indies had been brought dreadfully into
debt, and made subject to heavy mortgages. The compensation money has served to unlock the iron chests
and set the securities and title deeds free. Instead of
being subject, as formerly, to all the heavy charges of an
imperious consignee, imperious and unbending, because
the estates were under his power, the planter is now
at liberty to send his produce to the best market, to
choose for a correspondent the ablest merchant he can
find, and to bring the expenses of transport within the
utmost economical limits. One step in economy leads
to another: he looks about him on every hand:
pleased with the success of one experiment, he tries
another, and going on as a cautious, prudent man
ever will do, gets delivered from the consequences of
former poverty, neglect, and waste. The consequence
of the present state of things: of physical freedom to
the slave, and commercial freedom to the master, is this,
that landed estates are rising in value. The former
money-value of the slaves has already, in perhaps the
majority of instances, been transferred to the soil, many
properties in land now selling for a much larger sum,
than during the agitation of the slavery question the
land and the slaves would have sold for together.

What a practical comment on the adage, that justice is
in all cases the truest policy; and what an example to
those nations who, in spite of warning, and in defiance
of Christian principle persist in continuing slavery!

But if, instead of a pecuniary gain to the proprietor,
the planter should be able to prove a loss—if less sugar
and rum were likely to be exported, and the profits of
cane and coffee fields should sink to a minimum : what
would be the trifling inconvenience compared with the
immense advantages gained by the labouring community? The proprietary body has rather a smaller
income than before, but the people are well clothed,
housed, and fed; chapels and school-houses are erected,
education is sought after, public worship is frequented,
the prisons are getting gradually emptied, and a fine,
free, moral and religious peasantry tread the soil till lately
disgraced by fetters and the whip. Never was a great
moral experiment more successfully carried out than the
abolition of slavery in the British colonies; never, in
proportion to the number who were objects of it, was a
political change attended by such speedily happy results.
May England persevere in her righteous legislation till
every vestige of slavery has ceased from her soil in the
East as well as the West, and may her noble conduct
stimulate her daughter on the other side the Atlantic,
and all other nations to follow her example.

CHAPTER III.

RETURN TO HAYTI—SANTIAGO DE CUBA—TOWN OF CAPE
HAYTIEN—PLANTATIONS IN THE PLAINE DU NORD—
EXCURSION TO SANS SOUCI—CHRISTOPHE—GENERAL
OBSERVATIONS.

THE year 1840 had now nearly passed away, and the
employments which had so long detained us in Jamaica
being brought to a close, we took leave of our many
kind friends at Kingston, and went on board the
Government steamer bound for Barbados, with the
outward mail. The cabin passengers were seventeen
in number :—some bound for Cuba; two, like ourselves,
for Hayti; and the remainder for the windward isles,
or for Europe. The night was stormy, the wind
blowing hard a-head, but early the next morning we
lost sight of land, and at four o'clock, P.M., cast anchor
in the spacious and beautiful harbour of St. Jago.
The commander of the packet, knowing the remorse-
lessness of the Spanish character in these regions,
advised me not to go on shore, as since we landed
there twelve months before, a notification had been
made to the captains of English ships, that no person
known or suspected to favour missionary or anti-slavery
principles would be safe in the city, and that the
British Consul could not, if he would, afford them
protection. We felt no disposition to visit the city
again ; we had perambulated its streets once, and were

quite content to remain on deck, and take a leisurely
view of the shipping and the harbour, and the hills and
mountains that surround it. The dominion of slavery
may transform man into a monster, but throws no
curse on natural scenery. Commerce is ever active in
St. Jago: slaves on the quay and wharf, watched and
superintended by villanous looking white men and
half castes, are constantly busy in stowing away foreign
merchandise, and loading outward-bound vessels with
copper ore from the neighbouring mines. The city,
itself gloomy in appearance, like the bondage it fosters,
has streets of houses built after the Moorish fashion.
Heavy gateways open into court-yards, surrounded
by chambers and domestic offices : iron gratings
in front, instead of windows, frown on the street ;
jealousies above are substituted for curtains and blinds,
and broad piazzas on the second floor overhang the
pavement, protecting passengers from the rays of a
vertical sun. The streets are hot, unpaved, and dusty,
and in the middle of the day quiet enough ; some
common carts may be seen, and, perhaps, a few *volantes*
richly painted and gilded, with enormous high wheels,
and springs and axles so arranged as to adapt them to
deep gullies and broken ground, in which the wealthy
slave-owners, or their Creole ladies, without caps or
bonnets, ride out in a lolling careless posture to transact
business, or make their morning calls. At our first
visit to this port, in company with a young Peruvian,
our fellow-passenger, we called at the house of a bar-
rister, a friend of his, whose wife and daughter received
us with much courtesy. Almost as soon as we were
seated fruit was ordered, and when we had partaken
of it, a female slave entered the room with a pitcher of

water and basin, and a towel on her arm, and after
pouring water on our hands in succession, and handing
us the towel, removed the remainder of the feast,
and left the room. The inhabitants of Santiago are
estimated at from twenty-five to thirty thousand, of
whom a large number are household and out-door
slaves, in abject degrading servitude. We saw no
glass windows in a single house, except in the residence of the British Consul.

In the course of a few hours our commander received
the mail, and we again threaded our way amongst
the many vessels in the harbour, passed the castle of
Moro, and once more set sail in a stormy sea. The
threat now held out to missionaries and abolitionists who
dare to set foot on Cuban soil is, that "they shall be sent
to the Moro, and there lie without salvation." Another
rough night and swelling waves; but before noon on
the morrow we came in sight of Cape Nicholas Mole, in
Hayti, leaving the eastern coast of Cuba yet visible far
behind us. Early in the morning of the following day, we
landed a second time at Cape Haytien. It was the first
day of the new year 1841, the thirty-seventh anniversary
of Haytien independence, and of course kept as a
national festival. Liberty was proclaimed by Dessalines
—equal law and liberty to all classes in 1804. The
custom-house was closed, a sentinel or two watched the
landing of the passengers, and their luggage was sent
under guard to the public store. There are no taverns
in Hayti like those of Europe, where strangers are sure
to get accommodated for money; boarding-houses are
found in some of the larger towns, and where there
are none, the traveller must solicit board and lodging
as a favour, and grass for his horses if travelling on the

road, and get on in the best way he can. We obtained
private apartments at the Cape, at the house of La Veuve
Piquion, a respectable coloured matron, who keeps a
store on the quay, and is much esteemed by her neighbours for the prudent manner in which she trains up a
large family of sons and daughters. This good lady
received us as her guests, with liberty to dine alone, or
at a common table with herself and her children. For
the first few days we preferred the latter, and after that,
for several weeks used a common saloon with our friends
Henry and Maria W. Chapman, of Boston, Massachusetts,
who, advocates of anti-slavery principles like ourselves,
had come to this island to inspect the state and condition
of the people, to see the country, and improve their
health. At this house we were handsomely entertained,
with much satisfaction to ourselves, at a moderate cost,
and had no reason to repent our choice of a tavern. Let
not travellers from England and America expect, however, to find in Hayti well-furnished lodging rooms,
privacy of retirement, or those common comforts which
in their own ordinary family routine at home are considered as essential. They may depend on being supplied
with good food, and if they wish it, with the fine fruits
of the country, and the light wines of France: they
may find a lodging-room sheltered from the rays of the
sun, and the rains of heaven; more than these in the
shape of entertainment they must not look for. There
are many *discomforts* in Haytien domestic life, to which
only the mind naturally contented in itself can easily
become reconciled.

We had brought with us to this country some
large cases filled with elementary books for young
people, reading lessons for public schools, and a good

store of moral and religious works, chiefly in the
French and Spanish languages, which had been liberally
furnished by our friends in England. The duty on books
imported is very high in this island, amounting to
about twenty-five per cent. on the cost price; but when
I explained to the Director of the Customs that they
were brought for gratuitous distribution, and not as
merchandize, he generously allowed them to pass
duty free. This circumstance was the less expected
by us, and the more welcome, inasmuch as the British
Vice-Consul who had observed these cases in the
store, and know their contents, had told us we should
probably have much difficulty in getting them passed at
all. Our escape from trouble and cost on this occasion,
was partly owing to a young mulatto who had been in
Europe, and knew something of the religious society to
which we belonged, who told the sable chief he might
safely depend on our word. We are bound to bear
testimony to this act of kindness on the part of the
authorities, and to state that, in passing through the
island, we received everywhere from this and every other
class of public functionaries, polite and confiding attentions. Let not the white man, in the pride of his com-
plexion, look down with disdain on these black republicans : there are men in office in the island of Hayti,
both black and coloured, who would bear comparison
with men of the same class in any part of the world.
Having entered our names at the civil tribunal, and
promised submission to the laws of the state during our
sojourn, we were left at liberty to act as we pleased,
and to go anywhere within the limits of the Cape.
Whoever travels in the interior must procure a passport
from the General commanding the *arrondissement*.

The city of Cape Haytien, now for a time our residence, stands on the north-east side of a bay semicircled by hills of great elevation, such as in most countries would be called mountains. By these hills the extensive level district of " La plaine du Nord" is shut out from view. Standing on the quay, nothing strikes the eye but high land and wide ocean, except that at one point the level land leading to the mountains presents itself, and the glittering sea-side village of *La petite anse.* In former days, under the French dominion, this was considered the handsomest town of all the West Indies, and the most flourishing. It is still as large as ever, but half of it is in ruins, the public buildings and a large number of the houses having been battered down by cannon and musquetry, or destroyed by fire during the wars of the revolution, and never yet rebuilt. The pavement of some of the streets was broken up during the same dismal strife, or has since that period been ploughed up by the torrents which pour down from the mountains. The *toute ensemble* of the town, from these causes, has somewhat of a melancholy aspect, and gives the stranger at first view an unfavourable and rather gloomy impression. Its front towards the sea is nearly a mile in length ; and its breadth, backward to the hills, about three-quarters of a mile. Making allowance for all irregularities, Cape Haytien may be described as a city having twenty-seven streets, running east and west, crossed at right angles by nineteen others from north to south, containing what once were good houses, some of them magnificent, of two and three stories, built of brick or stone, and covered with slates, tiles, and mahogany or pine shingles. A wide gutter runs down the middle of each principal street, and con-

veys the mountain rains from the hills to the sea. In
general appearance, the place strikingly resembles St.
Pierre, of Martinique; both are built after the fashion
of France, and have their prototype in the more modern
towns of that country. The basement story of many of
the houses is occupied in stores, warehouses, and stables;
the upper part only being furnished as a residence for
the family. The population in 1789, amounted to
18,500; the present number of the inhabitants, including the small garrison, is supposed to be about nine
thousand. The cathedral is a handsome structure,
lately rebuilt by public subscription; the military hospital has been also of late restored, and improvements
are going on in other quarters. There are several handsome squares in the city, with fountains yielding good
water, but we looked in vain through them all for the
small temple commemorative of freedom, of which a
drawing is given by Rainsford in his ample quarto, and
which has been copied by the *Penny Magazine*, in a
sketch of the *Life of Toussaint L'Ouverture*, ascribed to
the pen of Harriet Martineau. There may have been
such a building, but it is not to be found here. The
trade of Cape Haytien is greatly decayed, though still
respectable. Much has been said of the salubrity of
Hayti, but the town and environs of the Cape afford
no proof of it. The rays of a vertical sun beaming
with full force are reflected by the hills behind, and
concentrated to a focus in the streets; added to which
there are marshes, and some low swampy land in the
immediate neighbourhood which yield at certain seasons
a pestiferous malaria. It is true, there are refreshing
winds blowing constantly from the sea in the day time,
which serve to moderate and temper the excessive heat,

and to dissipate the noxious air ; but the place, not-withstanding, must be unhealthy, especially after the heavy rains. During the military rule of Christophe, whom every body, when speaking of him, designates not as King, but as Monsieur, Cape Haytien was the capital of the island. This remarkable and very ambitious man began here the erection of a palace for himself, which was left unfinished at his death, and which now lies a desolation, as if to scoff at the pride of kingship, and level distinctions in the dust. On the western side of the town is a large open plain, called Le champ de Mars, where he used to exercise his troops. On this plain, during our stay at the Cape, we witnessed a review of the militia of the *arrondissement* or district, who are brought out once a quarter,for a single day. Early in the morning the drums were beating in every part of the city, and the soldiers, some on horseback, some on foot, clothed in dark military coats and white trowsers, not a precise uniform, were seen pouring in through the barrier, and sauntering to the place of rendezvous. At eight o'clock the square was formed. About two thousand foot soldiers, and three hundred horse, were mustered on the field. The commander, General Bottex, once in the confidence of Christophe, but now a sturdy republican, came to the ground with his field-officers, handsomely attired and mounted. Every officer had the accoutrements of his rank, and almost every charger was covered with a gay saddle-cloth. The troops were indiscriminately mixed of black and coloured, the latter bearing a proportion of perhaps two in ten. A con-siderable number of spectators made their appearance— women dressed in white and chintz, with gay turban Madras handkerchiefs, leading their children in holiday

garments; and many *young black gentlemen*, too young
to be yet in the ranks, came well dressed, with cane in
hand, or a handsome whip, riding on good ponies, with
yellow and puce coloured saddle-cloths, and pistol-cases
on their saddle-bows. The scene was gay and lively,
and seemed to afford much delight to the company
assembled; but it was speedily closed: the morning
proved unfavourable, a shower of rain came on, and the
General dismissed the troops before the review had well
begun. Every citizen of a given age not enrolled in the
standing army, or specially exempt by some profession,
is required to serve in the militia, and every individual
provides at his own cost his arms, clothing, and accoutrements. Great ridicule has been attempted to be cast on
the Haytien soldiery, who are represented in caricature
as so many scarecrows: their appearance on the present
occasion, except in the want of an exact uniform, was
nearly as respectable as that of an English brigade.

The only effectual employment of the soldiery in
Hayti, is that of an armed police: they drum and fife,
and muster on parade, and go through their evolutions,
but the country is in perfect peace, and they have
nothing to do, that tells for anything, but to stand
sentry at the doors of the public offices, and be ready
at the command of the magistrate to hunt up *les
mauvais sujets;* to guard prisons and prisoners who
work in the chain-gangs, and to loiter or lounge at the
barriers, collecting tolls and examining permits. One of
the most appalling sights at Cape Haytien is the groups
of criminals chained together, and sent into the streets
and suburbs to repair the roads and highways, accompanied by soldiers with loaded muskets. These poor
wretches are often ill fed and half naked, and some of

them gaunt and miserable, but happily their number is
not large. The *Public Prison* is a good building, with
spacious yards and clean apartments : it contained at
the time of our visit only forty sentenced prisoners.
The women are kept apart from the men, and the
debtors and convicts for petty offences have a ward to
themselves. The most hardened criminals who compose
the chain-gang, have a number of small rooms opening
into a close, narrow, common yard, which we were permitted to look into through a sort of wicket, but not to
enter, as we had no special order for this part of the
prison, and Captain Bottex, the Governor's son who kindly
conducted us, had no power to demand an entrance. Some
of the inmates were employed in plaiting grass and
rushes for baskets and mats, to eke out their miserable
subsistence of a few plantains weekly, others were quite
idle, and some nearly naked. The lunatics were kept
distinct from the criminals. This prison afforded us no
very favourable impression with regard to discipline, but
is probably quite as good as some of our English and
Irish prisons even at the present day. The *Military
Hospital* is a noble edifice, with large, long, well-venti-
lated, well-furnished apartments, and fitted up with a
good kitchen, and hot and cold baths. It contained but
sixteen patients, who appeared to have all the physical
comforts that men under their circumstances could desire.
There is a physician, a lay superintendent, and several
servants. The *Hospital for the Poor* is in a dilapidated
state and has few inmates. A society is formed to
endeavour to repair the buildings by public subscription,
and to make it an asylum worthy of a good city. We
had no reason to suppose from anything we saw or
heard, that much destitution or extreme poverty

prevails. There is in the negro race a spirit of kindness
not common to barbarous or half-civilised nations;
such is the testimony of Mungo Park and other African
travellers; and a disposition to help others is fostered
in this country by the influence of the Roman Catholic
religion, which teaches its votaries to rely on good works
as the ground of justification, and as meriting an eternal
reward. A few days before our arrival at the Cape, a
ship from Bremen with a hundred and seventy German
emigrants, bound for New Orleans, had been wrecked
at Point Isabella, and driven on shore in a heavy gale
of wind. No lives were lost; much damage was sustained, but the passengers and the crew were brought
in safety to the Cape. The news of their arrival—
strangers in a strange land, speaking an unknown
tongue, dejected, care-worn, much of their little property
lost in the wreck, some of them sick, and nearly all
without food—aroused the feelings of these good people,
and awakened the liveliest sympathy. No Consul of
their own nation to protect them, they might have
perished of hunger, but for the generous assistance of all
classes of the citizens. The authorities, all black or
coloured men, ordered houses to be open for their
reception, into which beds and moveables were conveyed; medical men proffered their assistance, and the
inhabitants supplied them with food and clothing. We
passed through some of the buildings where they were
placed, and were cheered to witness the alacrity with
which they were served. Their sorrows were soon
soothed by these kind attentions, and some of them, foregoing the pleasure which they had promised themselves
in an early meeting with their friends in Louisiana,
who had left their father-land before them, made

arrangements for a temporary sojourn in Hayti, where work at fair wages was promised them, and where they had found an asylum in distress. There are no poor laws in Hayti; assistance to the poor is voluntary; and from the abundance and cheapness of provisions, a small quantity of silver goes a great way. There is much reason to fear, however, that great suffering ensues from want of efficient medical help. The charges of medical men are not high, as in Jamaica and other of the islands; but owing to the little emulation that prevails among the people, and their consequent want of ready money, they are unable, especially in country places, to procure good advice and suitable medicines when needed. When an epidemic of an alarming character shews itself, a great mortality ensues. From this cause the increase of population is probably not larger in Hayti, where the soil is luxuriantly fertile, and where every man who is industrious, may by very little exertion procure all the common comforts of life, than it is in the old and crowded countries of Europe. It is very difficult, if not impossible, to judge of the healthiness or otherwise of particular districts from the mortality, owing to the extreme uncertainty of the number of deaths. Births are well registered, because almost every infant is brought to the priest to be baptised; but large numbers die and are buried in the country, of whom no notice is ever taken. A census is only taken in the town, and then in so imperfect a manner, as to leave the subject of population always in perplexity and doubt. The following is an abstract of the register of Cape Haytien :—

1839. Born 329. Died 349. Married —
1840. Born 353. Died 297. Married 32.

The deaths in this city, which is governed by a
Corporation and regulated by municipal laws, are said
to be accurately recorded : the number of inhabitants is
reported at something less than nine thousand. The
year of 1839, was one of great sickness ; but taking the
average of the two years, the births were as one in
twenty-five of the population—about the same average
as in England : the deaths as one in twenty-six, or
about fifty per cent. higher than in England. The
marriages are one in 266, or less than half the number
that take place in this country, and as a natural
consequence, a large proportion of the children born
are illegitimate. This statement, whilst it proves
nothing as to the general rate of increase in the whole
island, proves very decidedly that Cape Haytien is a
very unhealthy locality. This want of health among
the people cannot arise from bad dwellings, for the
houses are good and airy, and well fortified against the
influence of weather ; it must be attributed, as before
observed, to its situation at the foot of high hills,
reflecting the beams of a scorching sun, and from
swampy ground. But few of the merchants or principal inhabitants are married men : concubinage is
common, and unhappily, regarded as not dishonourable.
Whenever a ball is given, or a large party invited,
the invitation is equally extended to " Monsieur and
Madame ——," or to " Monsieur —— and his lady ;"
and by this confounding of moral distinctions among
the upper classes, the evil descends to the lower
ranks, and becomes perpetuated. Some of the merchants at the Cape are wealthy men, keep their country houses, and give handsome dinners, at which they
make a great display of servants, and costly plate :

they usually attend their stores and counting-houses during the day, and take their exercise on horseback an hour or two before sunset. Horses abound in the island, some of which are trained to great swiftness, and are always to be had at a moderate cost, either on purchase or hire. Not choosing to encumber ourselves with horses and servants during our limited stay, we hired two steeds which were to be always ready at our call, and in this manner, sometimes alone, sometimes accompanied by our friends from America, we explored the hills above the town, which afford many interesting rambles; and made sundry excursions to the sugar estates on the plain. One of the most agreeable journeys we made in this desultory manner was to Sans Souci, once the palace of King Henry Christophe, which lies at five leagues distance from the Cape along the level plain, and between a defile of hills, that form the termination of an extensive mountain range. General Bottex, the Commandant, had given us permission to visit it, as also the citadel. At three o'clock in the morning, the moon shining bright, the horses for our little company stood ready caparisoned at the door. Our good tempered laughing hostess, *La veuve Piquion*, a short fat personage, came out attired in a white muslin robe, with a damask silk shawl of crimson and white on her shoulders, and a yellow turban handkerchief on her head; the latter was surmounted by a new black beaver hat, surrounded by a broad golden band, bespangled in front by a golden star and buckle, and adorned with black plumes made to nod like a tuft of ostrich feathers. The back of her palfrey was spread over with a rich puce-coloured saddle-cloth, bordered with a fringe of gold lace: her second son, Francis

whom she had selected to be our guide, stood solemnly
by, with a long sword at his side, according to the
country phrase, " *pour nous debarasser des mechants ;*"
and as soon as he had seen the rest of us mounted,
sprung on his own saddle, which was adorned with
pistol cases, and led the way along the quay to the city
gate. My horse also was duly furnished with pistol
cases, covered with leopard skin, but without fire arms :
that of my wife was unincumbered. We presently
cleared *Le champ de Mars,* and came to the barrier.
The sentries were perhaps asleep, but the name of our
hostess, Piquion, loudly shouted, brought the officer
out who listened to the watch-word, or the tale she told
him, and the gate was opened. The rain a few days
before had fallen in torrents, and the road was, in some
places, so intolerably deep in mire, that we could only
pick our way slowly and by piecemeal, seldom exceeding a foot pace. About three miles from the city, we
met a curious group of country people in carts, and
with horses and asses loaded with yams, plantains, and
sweet potatoes, and some with bundles of guinea grass,
for sale at the morning market : they were bivouacking
by fire-light, sipping coffee, and waiting for the hour
when the city gate should be thrown open. The glare of
fire-light in the decaying moonbeams, on a company of
faces varying in colour from yellow brown to jet black,
and displaying teeth of ivory whiteness, produced a
singular effect. Soon after, we met other groupes,
some on foot, others on horseback ; the women riding
astride, like men, with infants in their arms, or asleep
behind them in apron folds at their back. Urchins of
boys, as is almost always the case in these expeditions,
ran before, or behind, and everywhere. " *Bon jour,*

Monsieur," " *Bon jour Madame*," were the cheerful
salutations that met our ear, accompanied, sometimes
by a sentence of unintelligible Creole, half French,
half African, that amused us from its oddity. The
people were dressed in common clothing; the women
in dark blue check, or printed cotton, with a Madras
handkerchief; the men in white jackets, or worn out
military coats; the children in an Osnaburgh shirt or
shift, some of them more than half-naked. The appearance of the men was rather ragamuffin, something like
that of a banditti. The common people of Hayti are
wonderfully docile, and free from the charge of attempts
at highway robbery, or we should not have wondered at
the strange fashion, for it is only a fashion, of going
armed through the country. It was once a common
custom in the Spanish part of the island, and is now
absurdly adopted on the French side. The roads we
passed over had hedges of the ordinary description, in
some places formed of the penguin aloe, or a plant with
sharp prickly pointed leaves, called Adam's needle; and
in others of logwood, which grows to a great height.
We passed by the massive gateways of many deserted
or neglected sugar estates, where the mansions that once
adorned them, are now crumbling and in ruins, shewing
the marks of their former destruction by fire, and subsequent decay. As the sun rose, we entered the defile
leading to Sans Souci, and as soon as we reached the
village, dismounted and ordered breakfast.

The Major-Commandant of the place had received
orders from the General to shew us respect. In consequence of the numerous books we had distributed, and
the attention we had paid to the public school, the
cognomen of philanthropists had been bestowed on

us at the Cape. A mounted cavalier came to the
door, and seeing me, a stranger, addressed our young
attendant with the question, *" Qui est ce Monsieur,
Le philanthrope ?"* *" Oui, le meme,"* was the reply.
Leaving his horse to the care of a soldier who stood
by, he immediately entered the house, introduced by
young Piquion, as *" Le Commandant de place."* Caught
in an undress, much, as we supposed, to his mortification, he could not assume the official consequence which
attaches, more particularly, to black officers in the
army. We sat together a few minutes, and I had good
leisure to survey his habiliments. Over a Madras
handkerchief wrapped tight round his head, like a man
suffering with a grievous cold, he had placed a large
cocked hat, which from its rusty colour, seemed to have
done service in the civil wars, twenty years before : the
nap, if it ever had any, was worn off, and a rent in the
front of it had been carelessly repaired by a kind of
packthread. The lace of his coat was tarnished;
sundry rents and gashes exhibited the lining : and his
trowsers, once of blue cotton or jean had been washed
to a dirty white. He was, however, vastly complaisant,
and we were very polite to each other. Was it our
pleasure to visit the citadel ? This we found would
have been too much to accomplish so as to return to
the Cape the same day : we therefore declined it, but
begged permission to visit the palace. He would conduct us himself to the palace of "Monsieur Christophe"
with great pleasure, and shew us whatever we wished
to see. A friend of his, Jacques Cæsar, a magistrate
and architect of the neighbouring chapel, who sat in the
room, requested leave to be one of the party. The
first view of Sans Souci from the village is very striking.

The palace stands between two lofty hills well covered with fine trees; and mountains rise on the back ground, on one of which the citadel stands. The buildings, though once splendid, were never in good architectural taste, and defaced as they now are from the battering of cannon and musket balls, windows shattered, walls crumbling, and the roof falling in, they resemble a huge deserted cotton factory. The whole domain, when properly maintained in the days of Christophe, must have been a princely affair, and adds one to the many other proofs he gave, that it was his ambition to be thought every inch of him a King. The rooms were spacious and lofty, the floors and side panels of polished mahogany, or beautifully inlaid with mosaic: the apartments are said to have been sumptuously furnished: and the gardens and the baths for the young princesses were all in keeping with the general splendour. The coach-houses and stables were magnificent. A number of the royal carriages still remain, the panels of which gilded and emblazoned by the royal arms, shew at how great a cost they must have been constructed. One of the coaches was built in London, and cost £700 sterling, and when equipped, as it used to be, with six fine grey horses and postilions on splendid saddles, bearing a King and his Chamberlain in their robes of state, must have struck the gazing negro crowd with astonishment. These splendid baubles are suffered by the present republican government to remain and moulder, and everything belonging to the palace to fall to decay, as a satire on the follies of kingship, and to render the name of King odious. The horse barracks in the vicinity of Sans Souci are deserted; and only a few straggling soldiers occupy the post. As soon as

the rebel troops heard that Christophe was dead, they
made an immediate furious attack on the palace: the
dead body of their monarch was treated with indignity,
scarcely saved from mutilation by a bribe from the
Queen; musketry was discharged through the windows
from the areas below; the secret chambers were ran-
sacked, and the treasures of gold and silver, of which
there was an ample booty, at once secured. The huge
mirrors that adorned the walls, in which—

> " He of Gath,
> Goliath, might have seen his giant bulk
> Whole without stooping, towering crest and all."—

were dashed to atoms. Everything within doors, and
everything without was exposed to the rapine and
fury of a soldier mob.

Christophe was the ruler of Hayti fifteen years. Born
in Grenada or St. Kitt's, (history is doubtful which) he
found his way to Cape Haytien when a very young
man, and entered early on a military life. Accepting
a commission under Toussaint L'Ouverture, he distin-
guished himself in many achievements; and when that
great and deeply injured man was betrayed and sent
prisoner to France, he made common cause with the
ferocious Dessalines to revenge, by renewed hostilities,
the perfidy of the French. At the death of Dessalines,
the northern army elected him chief of Hayti. He
never, however, obtained the rule of more than half the
territory of even that part of the island which had belonged to France; and the number of his subjects, when
King, probably never exceeded two hundred thousand.
Although he began his career with an evident desire
to improve the condition of the people, and give them

a standing among civilized nations, the maxims of his
government were unfortunately tyrannical. Wanting a
revenue, and not knowing how otherwise to obtain it,
and believing also that the people had become too
much dissipated by war to labour willingly for wages,
he compelled field labour at the point of the bayonet.
By this means, he secured large crops of sugar and rum;
and making himself, like Mohammed Ali of Egypt, the
principal merchant in his own dominions, he became
rich, kept a court, and maintained a standing army.
He took possession of the best plantations in his own
right, and gave others to some of his military comrades,
and a few civilians who pleased him, on whom he
bestowed the titles of Barons, Counts, and Dukes. The
Chateaux Royaux, as his own and the Queen's domains
were denominated, were worked by soldiers disbanded,
or on leave of absence. In the last year of Christophe,
twenty of these plantations yielded ten millions of
pounds of sugar, equal to 5000 hogsheads of a ton
weight each. One of them, three leagues from the Cape,
called the *Queen's Delight*, yielded 500 hogsheads of
superior sugar, of the enormous weight of 25 cwt. each.
Many of the estates of his great men were cultivated
like his own, by coerced labour. Liberty did not at
once obtain dominion in Hayti. The black army had
triumphed; but the black generals forgetting the pit of
slavery from whence they had emerged, exercised but
little mercy, and showed but little regard to their
companions in arms who had fought under them in the
ranks. Over this part of the history of the Haytien
revolution, philosophy and humanity might gladly draw
the veil.

Christophe and Pétion were political rivals, and a

murderous war of some years was carried on between them. Buoyant at first with success, Christophe became soured in after life through repeated disappointments. Possessing great powers of mind, he resolved on great enterprises, and having once undertaken a project would suffer no controllable difficulty to interrupt its progress. The citadel of La Ferriere had been begun by the French : he determined to carry out the design, and make it one of the strongest fortresses of the world. I asked Captain Agendeau of Cape Haytien, who worked two years and a half as a prisoner within the walls, how many persons had lost their lives by hard labour during its erection ? " As many persons," he replied, " as there are stones in the building : every stone cost the life of a human being." This famous citadel was reared by bands of men and women, who were compelled to labour on very insufficient rations of food : vast numbers died in consequence of exhaustion, and many more of wounds and bruises received in the cruel work of forcing stones and other heavy materials up the steep sides of the mountain. Prisoners were employed upon it. Captain Agendeau was sent there, with thirty-two other coloured men, out of revenge for the escape of two mulattos who had gone to join Pétion's army at Port-au-Prince. Christophe had a strong and invincible prejudice against the coloured class, of whom Pétion was one. The coloured people were aware of it, both men and women; and endeavoured, it is believed, by secret counsels, to effect his overthrow. On his return to Sans Souci, on one particular occasion, he was informed that during his absence, the mulatto women of Cape Haytien had offered up prayers in the great church that he might never be permitted to return again to his palace: revenge rankled in his soul—his purpose was immediately taken—he ordered a company of his soldiers to make domiciliary visits, and lead out the accused women to summary execution. A dark retired spot, about a mile from the city was chosen for the massacre; and here in cold blood these unhappy victims of cruelty were butchered. Bayonets were plunged into their bosoms, and their dead bodies cast into a deep well; this well is now called, *The Well of Death*, and nobody will drink of its waters. We took a walk to the place with one of the citizens, who assured us that there was scarcely a coloured family at the Cape who had not to mourn a near relation, lost to them in that horrid catastrophe. Many other acts of Christophe's cruelty and tyranny were related to us by eye and ear witnesses. Not an individual in the north of Hayti affects to doubt of his tyranny, or attempts to palliate his misdeeds. A respectable merchant, who when young served in the citadel, assured us, that the King on rising early one morning proceeded to the hospital, and finding that the French physician whom he had engaged to attend the troops had not yet made his appearance, sent for him, and gave him a severe reprimand; high words ensued—the King ordered him to be beaten—the physician, indignant at this treatment, said, " You have dishonoured me; you may as well take off my head at once." "Do you desire that?" said Christophe, " your wish shall be gratified;" an immediate order was given to his guards: the culprit was led into a near apartment, and his body presently brought out a headless trunk. One of Christophe's generals was a black man, (we conceal his name, though it is, well

c 3

known in Hayti) who having heard of the orders
given to destroy the mulatto women at the Cape,
inhumanly killed his own concubine, who was one of
the number, and his child. One day, when in company
with the King, hoping to obtain his favour from the
circumstance, he related what he had done. The
monarch, for once, seemed horror-struck ; anger flashed
in his dark face, and whirling his baton at the General's
head, he knocked out one of his eyes. This very officer
—this executioner of his most intimate friend, this literal
" *monstrum horrendum cui lumen ademptum*," passed
over to the republican side, when President Boyer
made his triumphal entry at the Cape, and now com-
mands an *arrondissement* in the eastern part of the
island ! The fact here given was related to us, both in
the north and south by different individuals. One fact
more, and we shall close for the present our catalogue
of crime. Leaving Sans Souci one morning for the
Cape, in a carriage drawn by his beautiful greys, the
road being miry from a heavy shower of rain, the
wheels stuck fast in the mud; the angry chief descended
from his carriage, and with his own hand, as the story
was told us, hamstrung the horses with his sword, and
laid a contribution on the citizens at Cape Haytien to
the value of the horses, for not having kept the road in
repair ! These and similar freaks and crimes, were the
outbursts of a semi-barbarian mind, untutored, undis-
ciplined, but formed by nature for great purposes, and
endowed with extraordinary gifts. This great man,
for great he was as well as cruel, had the sagacity to
see that nothing but education could raise the mass of
his subjects from the heathen ignorance and degradation
into which slavery had plunged them. He resolved,

therefore, on establishing schools for boys and a college;
and his purposes for good, as well as for evil, being
always acted on with energy, he addressed letters to the
philanthropists of England, invited over competent
masters, built school rooms, imported books and lessons,
set up printing presses, and began the good work of
education for this class of his subjects, with a diligent
unsparing hand. The education of girls was wholly
neglected. Few schools were set up at first, or indeed
at any time, in the rural districts; but one at least was
established in every town. The common branches of
elementary education were taught, together with the
English language, which he vainly hoped might be
made to supersede the French, and the mathematics.
Young men were trained at the college to serve as
engineers, physicians, and classical instructors. Several
of the schools are now extinct, but the fruits of them
remain; the encouragement thus given to learning has
had its influence on Haytien society to the present day.
Several civilians and officers of the army, who were
taught in these schools, are men of capability and
intelligence, and speak the English language fluently;
they venerate our country, and our tongue remains
an object of study and emulation to their children.
Christophe was not only the patron of education but
of industry; and it gave him pleasure to see his country
recovering the ' ground lost in the civil wars, and
advancing in name and wealth. He promoted industry
on the principles laid down by his predecessor,
Toussaint, but went far beyond him in urging the
severities of the rural code: this among other things
tended to render him unpopular; and when remon-
strated with by Sir Home Popham, the English Admiral

who came on a visit to him from Jamaica, he justified himself on the ground that he understood best the character of his own people, and that decision, firmness, and severity were indispensable. He desired also, and earnestly promoted the extension of legitimate commerce, which he followed up very much after the manner of the present Pacha of Egypt; and had many points in his character which would have made him to rank high among rulers, had not ambition and tyranny marred the great and generous qualities which really existed in his mind. Tyranny, during the last few years of his life was his ruling infirmity, and led to his overthrow. A beginning mutiny had broken out at St. Mark : he gave orders to the garrison at the Cape to march out immediately, seize the ringleaders, and put them to death. "Let us rather go to Sans Souci," said the officers, "and cut off his own head." " I am ready to join you," said the Duke de Marmalade. A largess was given to the soldiers, and they marched toward the palace. The King learned too late the extent of the conspiracy, and felt at once that his reign was ended : he was sick at home unable to mount his horse; and ordering all who were about his person to leave the room, he took a pistol, and deliberately shot himself dead. Such was the end of this negro chief; a man, who in the beginning, and in some subsequent stages of its career, seemed likely, under Divine providence, to prove a blessing to Hayti. His aims were great, and many of them good, but being mixed with turbulence and passion, they brought misery to many of his subjects, and proved of little advantage to the people whom he governed. In one respect, he excelled Charlemagne; he could write his own name, but

this, as far as the art of writing went, is said to
have been the extent of his accomplishment.   He
dictated letters and despatches, and was an admirable
judge of the fitness and relevancy of words.   His
private secretary was the Baron de Vastey, a mulatto,
a man of respectable literary acquirements, as his
history of Hayti shows, but of a base dishonourable
disposition.

On returning from Sans Souci to the Cape, we took
a new road by *La grande riviere* and *Le quartier
Morin*, passing through the midst of many fine sugar
plantations, either deserted, or cultivated only in part
by a few labourers, who work on the system recognised
by the *Code rurale*, and now in general use, of receiving
one-quarter of the net produce, with provisions to live
on, or half the produce without.   Among the plantations we noticed in the course of the day, were the
following, Praderés, Camfort, Gerbier, Charrier, Le
Pont, Fontinelle, Icé, Lacombe, Lalande, Carré, Sans
Souci, and Duplas.   The plantation Icé belongs to La
veuve Belliard, where we stopped and conversed with
some of the shipwrecked emigrants who had here obtained employment, and were just sat down in one of the
large outbuildings to a substantial repast.   Lacombe is
the property of Jacques Cæsar, the intelligent magistrate
and architect, who accompanied us through the ruined
apartments of the palace, and who persuaded us to pay
him a hasty visit at his own home.   We could not fail
here to be struck with the entire equality that seems now
to subsist in Hayti between servant and master.   Every
workman that made his appearance was addressed in
the courteous language, " *Mon fils,*" and on inquiring
the cause, we found it to be that the profits of planting

were good, labourers were scarce, and that it was necessary to conciliate all by kindness, or no work would be
done. Good land may be had of the government in
every part of the island at a low price; and any man
not satisfied with his condition as a private labourer,
may easily buy it, and become a freeholder in his own
right. The slave cabins of a former proprietor remained
on Lacombe, and were tenanted by the labourers, who
work in common, as joint sharers with the proprietor of
the produce. These cabins or houses, like many others
that we saw on other plantations are something better
than those of Jamaica; but the people in general are not
so well clothed, and some of the children are quite
naked. The peasantry of Hayti, through the prevalence
of heathenism and ignorance, have little emulation, and
few wants, and grow up contented with common fare,
coarse clothing, and enjoyments of a mere animal
nature: it is true, they work to live, as without some
labour they cannot subsist; but they do not, and they
will not work hard to please anybody, and hence
agriculture languishes, and commerce is stationary.
Duplas is one of the many plantations denominated
Chateaux Royaux, formerly cultivated by Christophe
for his own personal benefit, and is now in possession of the President Boyer. There is on it a
handsome mansion, and some very respectable storehouses, a distillery, and a large number of very good
cabins. The maxims of government adopted by
Boyer, are in many respects totally opposed to
those of Christophe: he neither compels labour by
military coercion, nor holds out higher inducements of
a pecuniary nature than his brother planters; hence his
estates, like theirs, are only half cultivated, and exhibit

signs of neglect. The guava bush covers what once were cane-fields, and diminished herds of cattle roam over the pastures. On reaching the handsome village of Morin, we dismounted at the Vicar's house; he was not at home, but his sister, a Spanish lady, brought us out cassava, bread, and sweet cakes, and offered us wine and lemonade. Having rested a while in their spacious cool keeping-room, and taken a walk through the cemetery, we hastened on our journey homewards, fearful that the sun might set before we reached the Cape, and leave us in total darkness. The town of La Petite Anse stands on a bay that fronts the town of Cape Haytien. In passing through it, several groups of women and children respectably attired, some of them handsomely, came to the doors of their houses to greet us. We were much struck with their agreeable appearance; and that of the place in general. Devastation has done its work here in past days; many of the buildings were set on fire, or destroyed by cannon, and are still in ruins, but many remain in a good condition. The road from *Petite Anse* to the Cape is on the shore, washed by the waters of that awful bay, where in the time of Le Clerc and Rochambeau, the French army made such a dreadful havoc of their prisoners of war, sending them out heavily ironed in boats and plunging them into the sea! Many a sumptuous banquet of human flesh have the sharks enjoyed on this coast, and the sight of its waters is constantly recalling the horrors of those dreadful days. Can Europeans reproach Dessalines, Christophe, and their black armies with cruelty? Let them look at the conduct of their own savage military commanders, and see on which side cruelty the most predominates. How gladly

should we draw the curtain of night over transactions
that disgraced the world! Wearied with our long
day's excursion, gratified by what we had seen of the
country and the people, but far from gratified with
recitals which we heard, or which history, speaking to
us on the very spots where dark deeds were done,
recalled to our recollection; we passed over the ferry
which led to our lodgings, and retired to rest.

On excursions of this kind, though not so long, we
often set out accompanied by our friends from Boston,
and explored the immediate environs of the Cape. We
visited villages and solitary houses together on hill and
plain, conversed with the common people whom we met
on the road or at their own houses, looked at their provision grounds and gardens, and obtained an acquaintance with their mode of life. A feeling of sympathy
for the past wrongs of Hayti, and for the negro still
held in unrighteous bondage in many parts of the
western world, bound us together in a common cause,
and a grateful companionship; often did we congra-
tulate each other on what we saw of the freedom and
physical happiness of those who were once slaves in
this land, but who are oppressed no longer. Nor did we
omit often to advert to that debasing servitude in which
millions of the negro race are still held in the United
States, by a people calling themselves Christians, and
boasting of their country as the freest on the earth!
What a mockery of religion was once the conduct of
Great Britain towards the slaves in her colonies : what
a mockery of religion is the present conduct of America ;
and what a lie to the declaration of her federal constitution, that all men by nature are free and equal! The
single circumstance that we were all sincere haters of

the abominable system of slavery in all its forms, and under every modification, ensured us a cordial reception in Hayti, and made our stay there, so far as it depended on the authorities, and the good wishes of the people, highly agreeable to us.

One object of our continued stay at the Cape was to ascertain, as far as possible, the moral and religious state of the people there; and with this view we visited the public and private schools, and sought interviews with the Romish priests and the few Protestant missionaries, who from different parts of the country—from Port-au-Prince, Port-au-Platte, Samana, and from Turk's Island, of the Bahamas—had come there to hold their annual conference. The high school of Cape Haytien was founded by Christophe in 1816, and is conducted on the monitorial system : the lessons used are those of the Borough Road School, and the Scriptures without comment are used as a class-book. The master has a salary from the government of seventy Haytien dollars per month, equal in the present depreciated currency to £63 sterling per annum, and is allowed the liberty of receiving a few private pupils on his own account, who pay him about fifty shillings each per annum for instruction. The average attendance of boys is 135 daily, who are engaged in study seven hours a-day, during five days of the week. The pupils are well instructed in the common branches of learning, and are taught to think, to exercise the memory, and to behave politely. Some of the forwardest of the boys are taught the English language by a Creole professor who speaks it well. Children of African descent excel in the imitative arts, and hence they write a good hand; the specimens of penmanship we saw in this school

were admirable. The management of it altogether—the
quietness—the docility of the boys—their reading, and
their compositions, would reflect credit on any institution
of the sort in any country. Besides this school, there are
in the city seven private schools for boys, averaging
forty pupils each; and nine for girls, averaging fifteen
each. There are also four professors, or tutors, who
give lessons to about fifty children at their own homes.
The total number of children of both sexes receiving
education at the Cape is about 550, or one-sixteenth of
the entire population : about half as many in proportion
to the population as receive education in *the towns* of
Jamaica. The difference between these two islands in
regard to education is very great. In Jamaica, schools
are fast spreading over the whole country, and begin
to act beneficially on the rural population ; in Hayti,
they are confined exclusively to the towns, and in the
country, where at least seven-eighths of the population
is to be found, there is as much ignorance as in the
days of slavery.

The middle class among the citizens are exceedingly
attached to stage entertainments. There is a public
theatre at Cape Haytien, and so widely does the folly
spread, that those schools are most encouraged in which
the young people are taught to act plays. A sort of
rehearsal takes place occasionally, and the parents and
friends of the pupils attend to witness and applaud.
But little religious instruction is imparted at the private
schools, and that little is exclusively Roman Catholic.
A large number of the men who live in the towns of
Hayti, as is said to be the case in many other popish
countries, are unbelievers ; the women attend mass
frequently, and confession at least once in the year; and

flock to the Cathedral on high days, attired in holiday
dresses, presenting a gay and attractive spectacle. The
usual dress of the upper class of women on these occasions, is a handsome robe of chintz or white muslin, a
turban handkerchief folded gracefully on the head, gold
and pearl ornaments on the neck, silk stockings, and
satin shoes. Gay silk parasols or umbrellas are their
constant accompaniments. The dress of the men is very
similar to that of England and France; but persons in
office, whether civil or military, frequently bear a gold-
headed baton which they use as a walking-stick, or
handle, with an air of official dignity.

One Protestant missionary, and only one, is settled at
the Cape: he, like all the rest of the Wesleyan persuasion,
has a small congregation, and preaches alternately in
French and English. The state of Protestantism is de-
plorably low in every quarter of the island, the religious
services of the missionaries, who are Englishmen, being
chiefly attended by coloured people who emigrated from
America, and were nominally Protestants before they
came. The congregations at all the stations are small,
and very little disposition is evinced by any class of the
people to send their children to a Protestant school, even
for gratuitous instruction. Satan, the grand deceiver,
wears in this land of moral darkness a four-fold face—
infidelity, ignorance, heathen superstition, and a religion
(as taught by many of the priests) of folly and lies.
One or other of these qualities may be said to frown in
every quarter. The sight is appalling, but nothing will
terrify the devoted follower of Christ, or deter him
from endeavouring to convert his deluded fellow-men
from blindness and error. The pure and peaceable principles of the gospel have won their way in regions

darker than this, and will yet prevail even here. The influence and success of Protestant missions is not at first to be judged of by the number only of those persons who attend at a stated religious service. The missionary mixes with the people out of doors, converses familiarly with them, distributes tracts, bestows useful books, settles differences, and gives encouragement to the well-disposed : his wife helps him in his labour of love to the people, joins him in setting a good example, and shows many acts of kindness and assistance towards her own sex. Not putting their light under a bushel, but on a candlestick, they give light to their neighbours around them, and win them gradually to examine and see for themselves, what the root is from which these Christian virtues spring. Faith bids us to believe that true Christianity will yet make its way by its own resistless energy, and the blessing of its Divine Author, through every region of the globe.

The government of Hayti assumes the power of appointing the priests to their respective cures, and of shifting them at pleasure from place to place. Some of the most respectable for character and learning are placed in the larger towns. The Curé of Cape Haytien is a Spaniard ; his assistant, or vicar, is a Frenchman— an Abbé by title, and a man of more than common endowments of mind. The latter ecclesiastic, obligingly made us a call soon after we landed; I gave him a copy of most of the publications we intended to distribute : he promised to look them over; had no objection, he said, to the propagation of any works which tended to promote our common Christianity, but must resist all books of a controversial nature, aimed point-blank at the Church of Rome. Our books were not generally of

this sort, though strictly evangelical in their scope and
tendency : some of them he recommended to his
parishioners, and during our stay interdicted none of
them. He frequently called on us, and we returned
his visits. Our conversation turned on subjects of a
moral and religious nature, connected with the welfare
of the people. On one occasion, speaking of a book
intended to illustrate the religious principles of the
Society of Friends, he remarked, that they laid no stress
on good works as the ground of our justification and
acceptance with God, and that they admitted only one
baptism as essential—that of the Holy Ghost and of
fire; on both these points he thought they were in
error : on both the Catholic Church differed widely
from them, and the Catholic Church, he presumed,
was right. With regard to the first question, that of
justification by works, I endeavoured to show him
that this was the very point on which the reformation
by Luther turned—that Protestants look to faith
in Christ, a faith that works by love to the purifying
of the heart, as the alone ground of a sinner's justification before God ; and that Roman Catholics, by adopting
the opposite principle of salvation by works alone, make
fallen man his own justifier and not Christ : so that by
this system Christ may be said to have died in vain.
With regard to water baptism, which the Church of
Rome regarded as a sacrament, I argued that as the
work of man's purification could be effected only by
the cleansing power of the Holy Spirit, which was the
washing of regeneration, " the baptism that now saves,"
according to the testimony of the Apostle Peter himself,
and as the Friends admitted this baptism in all its
fulness as essential, subscribing to it *ex animo*, he must
not place them out of the pale of Christianity, because

they differed from him in a ceremonial rite. He allowed, with regard to justification, that he had not so entirely made up his mind as to refuse to re-consider the question, and promised to come again and renew our discourse. Before we quitted this part of Hayti we called to take leave of him, and found him reading Barthe's *Annales de L'eglise*, a copy of which we had given him. He said he saw no reason why the holy Scriptures should be interdicted to the laity; and was so far touched with a feeling of protestantism, that he requested me to give him an introduction to the Paris Bible Society, and consented at last to allow me to order for him fifty copies of De Sacy's French Bible, an approved Roman Catholic version, and two hundred copies of his New Testament for a beginning distribution among his flock. The Abbé is a man of polished exterior, speaks elegant French, and from having lived much in Paris, and mixing evidently with good society, is an interesting, agreeable companion. He gave us at parting his hearty benediction in the few expressive words, *Dieu vous protege*.

The books which we brought for distribution made a great noise; we were, in fact, so besieged by applications for them, that we began to fear our hostess would look upon our vocation, as a nuisance. There are no booksellers' shops in the city; the few works that are sold are disposed of at the general stores, and consist chiefly of dictionaries and other school books, with a few Romish prayer books, and fabulous church legends.

The time which we had proposed to stay at Cape Haytien having drawn to a close, we made application to General Bottex for a passport, and made preparations for a journey by land to the town of Gonaives, on the western coast of the island.

CHAPTER IV.

DEPARTURE FROM CAPE HAYTIEN—JOURNEY TO GONAIVES
—TOWN AND COMMERCE OF GONAIVES—COASTING
VOYAGE TO PORT-AU-PRINCE.

HAVING made a bargain with one of the citizens for
two good saddle horses, together with a sumpter horse
to carry our little baggage, and a servant to attend us :
we despatched our other effects by sea, and waited the
hour of departure. For the accommodation thus agreed
on, we paid eighty Haytien dollars, or £6 sterling; it
being stipulated that we should make the journey to
Gonaives in two days, and that the servant should feed
himself, and take care of the horses by the way. The
distance was seventy miles. But, alas! for bargains;
and, alas! for carefully made arrangements in a strange
land, and among a people of strange tongues. The
servant confided to us as an honest man and good guide,
spoke a barbarous Creole dialect, half French, half
African; and his only object being to save a few dollars
for himself, he would have half-starved the poor horses,
if we had not discovered his trickery, and bought grass
for them out of our own purse. Being well mounted
ourselves, on animals that we had tried before : we set
out in good spirits, and soon outstripped our lazy
attendant. Our journey for the first six leagues to
Limbé, was over the *Plaine du Nord*, by a grand
broad road, flanked for a great part of the way on

each side by plantations and well cultivated provision
grounds. The houses on the plantations, once inhabited
by the owners, were nearly all in ruins, and the estates
much neglected; the outbuildings also were much
dilapidated. We passed on the edge of the fine estate
where Toussaint L'Ouverture was born, and from
which he made his escape when a slave, to lend a hand
to the rebel troops. On ascending the hill which led
to Limbé, we had a beautiful view of the river, the
bay, the ocean; the country was wonderfully picturesque and afforded us delight. The town of Limbé is
situated on rather high ground, and consists principally
of two long streets and a public square. The inhabitants are about five hundred, chiefly small freeholders,
subsisting on the produce of their own grounds. The
houses are better than the common huts of plantations,
plaster-built, wattled, and thatched, and stand apart
from each other, having many of them a small garden
attached, in which were bread-fruit trees, orange trees,
plantains, and bananas. One of these gardens, three
hundred feet by sixty-five, yields the owner a large
supply of provisions and small vegetables, and three
hundred pounds of coffee annually. We called on
Colonel Cincinatti, the Commandant, who received us
very politely. This military officer was once chamberlain to King Henry Christophe, and possessed the
manners of a courtier. Kindly offering my wife his
arm, he conducted us through the place, showed us all
that was worthy of observation; and invited us to make
free use of his dwelling-house as long as we should
think proper to stay. We thanked him for his
proffered hospitality; but were obliged to take leave at
an early hour. Our servant whom we had left behind

reached the town before we left it; but finding that
no dependence could be placed on his keeping up with
us, we engaged a new guide, and pressed on to Camp
Coq, a village situated in a defile of the mountains,
three leagues distant. We saw numerous habitations
by the road-side, and abundant indications of a rising
and thriving population. We met several groups of
people; women riding on horseback like men, and
many naked children. The men of Hayti pass much
of their time in sauntering, idling, talking, and playing
games of chance or skill: some we saw stretched out
at their ease under the shade of trees; others were
sitting on chairs and stools in the open air, as if they
had nothing to do, and were only desiring to kill time.
Most of the women were pretty well dressed; but many
of the men, like others we had seen at the Cape, were
clothed in a ragged military uniform, which had done
its service on parade, and was thought too good to be
thrown away. We had taken the precaution on leaving
the Cape to pack up a cold roasted fowl, on which, with
an omelet prepared by a cottager, and a cup of coffee,
we had breakfasted by the way; but the evening drew
near, and we wanted dinner. The village of Camp
Coq is the only convenient resting-place between Cape
Haytien and Gonaives; and here, according to information given us, we expected to find good entertainment
and handsome lodging. On reaching the place, our
guide stopped short at a poor hut, got off his horse and
told us to dismount. "We are not going to stop here,"
said I, "this cannot be the house." "Oui Monsieur,
c'est ici que demeure Madame Babilliers." There was
no alternative; we had really arrived at the far-famed
tavern, and reluctantly entering, prepared to pitch our

D

tent for the night. Our saddles were removed, and the horses turned out to grass: we paid off the guide, and ordered our evening meal. Our hostess, poor as was the house she lived in, really understood her business, and made us welcome. In about two hours, we sat down at a table covered with a nice clean table-cloth, napkins and silver plate, to a good dinner, consisting of soup, stewed fowl, rice, yams, and plantains, and graced with a bottle of claret wine. The next point of consideration was the lodging: this was less suited to our taste and wishes. The hut was divided into three apartments: the middle was the dining room, with a clay floor worn into deep holes: the two sides were portioned off as lodging-rooms by thin walls, that reached to within a few feet of the naked thatched roof, and afforded ample room for scorpions, lizards, and snakes. The mattress for visitors was good and clean. We had scarcely retired to seek such rest as the place might afford, when there came up to the house a troop of travellers, to claim, like ourselves, the benefit of a night's shelter—twenty men, women, and children, with a number of loaded asses. Nothing dismayed, and thinking only of the small gratuity she should receive for each, the good lady, our hostess, took them all in. The asses were tethered near the door, or let loose on the common: some of the men laid themselves down in the piazza with a slight covering over them: the rest of the company, of both sexes, spreading mats on the dining-room floor, sought repose there. Before attempting to sleep, they lighted some candle wood, smoked tobacco out of short pipes, talked, laughed, and sung, and were very merry. The asses brayed, and till about midnight we could get no rest; between that

time and early cock-crow we obtained some sleep, and
then rose to pursue our journey. It was three o'clock,
and our departure gave rise to a general commotion:
coffee was prepared for us at a side table; and to reach
it we had to pass over, or through, the medley crowd of
lodgers on the floor. Some of the women sprang up,
lighted candle wood, as on the evening before, and
began to smoke; others lifted themselves up with a
sort of laughing astonishment, to gaze on as we sipped
the coffee, and to hear us give directions for the journey.
Our new guide, whom we had hired the day before,
stood by, with a long sword girt close to his side. The
most comical part of the scene was to come. We had
looked at the drowsy visitors coiled up on the floor,
and observed the singular effect of a dull light on
dusky skins with some amusement; but presently, our
landlady, who had been very attentive to us, came up
to the coffee stand, to present her bill. I drew out my
purse, and gave her a small gold coin and some of the
debased silver coin of the country. She had probably
never looked on a piece of gold before, and evidently
wondered what it could mean: I explained its value,
and my statement was confirmed by a stander by: she
looked at it on both sides, turned it over, and over, and
over again: her very soul seemed fixed on the coin, as
though it was meant to deceive her; and at last, utterly
incredulous as to its worth, she refused to take it, and
returned it into my hands. What a subject was here
for the pencil of a Rembrandt! The light of two
candles concentrated on a yellowish bronze face worked
up by the spirit of covetousness, from a fear of losing
its due, and a group of people, old and young, white,
black, brown, and yellow, standing, sitting, or lying

around, in a dull, dusky cabin. Our baggage, which
contained a bundle of dollar notes, was already packed
up; we opened it again, took out some paper, and left
it with her to her heart's content.

We were now at liberty to take leave of Camp Coq,
and again mounted our horses. Our company was now
five persons : my wife and I, our servant from the Cape,
a friend of his whom he had picked up by the way, and
a guide, who knew the neighbourhood, and could conduct
us in the dark. Confidence in the common people of
Hayti is rarely or never misplaced; strangers may travel
in every part of the country, night and day, without
danger of being robbed or molested. Our journey led
us through mountain streams, over rocky and rugged
ground : the stars afforded us sufficient light where no
tall trees overshadowed the road; but we came to several
passes where bamboos had been planted on both sides,
which, bending down, formed a dense-arched canopy
over our heads, and made the road as dark as a railway
tunnel. Through avenues of this sort the river in
some places flowed : the bottom of the stream was
stony, and it seemed hardly safe for my wife to venture
through on horseback, lest a false step of the animal
should plunge her in the water : at these spots, therefore, one of the black guides took her in his arms, and
waded with her to the opposite bank, leaving another
to conduct the horse; and thus by dint of patience,
courage, and confidence, we got safely along, and met
with no disaster.

At sun-rise a morning mist veiled the sides of the
mountains, and filled the valleys like a mighty river:
the summits of the hills were clothed with luxuriant
vegetation; but the gorges between, and the villages

scattered on their slopes were hid from view; as
day advanced, and the sun increased in power, the
mists gradually disappeared : clouds of vapour rolled
up the mountains, dissolving above them into thin
air; the banana, the cabbage palm, the tree fern, and
the graceful bamboo disclosed their beautiful forms;
huts and provision grounds emerged to view; and
sheep, goats, and cattle, seemed suddenly to spring into
existence and to gladden the green fields. The air
was sufficiently cool to allow of active exercise; and
descrying, from the top of a hill, the town of Plaisance
at about a league distant; we set off at a brisk canter,
to reach it as soon as possible to obtain a wished-for
breakfast. On arriving, we inquired for a place of
entertainment, and found, to our dismay, that there was
none in the place : the only alternative, therefore, was
to throw ourselves on the charity of some good house-
holder, and to send the guides on a scamping expedition
to procure forage for the horses. One of the public
officers, a sort of deputy-major, kindly received us, and
desired his wife to prepare us eggs, coffee, bread and
milk. Entertainments of this sort, though highly
welcome to travellers, are more expensive than the
common and better repasts of an inn or boarding-house;
as the mistress looks for a consideration far exceeding
the value of the benefit conferred on her guests.

We here paid our respects to the black general, Dubat;
and after surveying the market, and calling at a few
houses to converse with the inhabitants, we proceeded on
our route with a new guide; leaving the servant, with
his friend and the baggage to follow. The mountains of
Plaisance, about 3000 feet in height, have many attrac-
tions of climate and scenery: they abound in small coffee

plantations; the palm and fern-trees grow luxuriantly
tall; and fruit trees are abundant. The commune, (or
parish) of Plaisance gave a title in Christophe's days to
one of his dukes. The road which hitherto had been
good, soon after leaving the town, became narrow, steep
and stony; giving warning of our approach to the far-
famed and magnificent pass of Les Escaliers; the ladder
or staircase descent which leads to the plains below. On
arriving at the brow of the mountain, we looked down
on a long, steep, smooth road, paved with flat stones,
many of them broad like a London pavement, and from
constant wear become almost as slippery as glass itself.
A mule of the Andes would look at such a pass for a
few moments, place its fore feet in a right position,
adjust its body to its burden, give a loud snort, and
slide down with rapidity. Our horses were not suited
to this sort of enterprise, and we had no courage for
the feat. What should we do? There was another
road winding through the lower country, longer by four
leagues; this seemed too far: we therefore resolved to
go on, taking all chances, and dismounting, led the
horses as well as we could, and with a little sliding, but
without a fall or bruise, brought them safely down the
steep. Truly thankful were we at last to find ourselves once more on secure ground. The sides of this
strange road are defended, in many places, by massive
granite rocks, and adorned in others by magnificent forest
trees and deep woods. The scenery is grand, but the
way perilous. To strangers circumstanced as we were,
with horses not absolutely to be depended upon as sure-
footed, the only alternative was to dismount and walk;
the thought that we escaped danger by doing so, served
to keep up our spirits, and enabled us to endure the toil.

We now look back on our descent of *Les Escaliers*
with vivid pleasure; but we had to pay for it at
the time by a sense of weariness that left us less able
to cope with the fatigues that followed. The day
was sultry : a vertical sun beamed full on our heads,
and there was no place of entertainment or shelter near.
At length, after several hours of toil, we came to a good
looking habitation, enclosed by wooden fences; and
we turned in to solicit food and rest. The first object
that met our view was a naked mulatto girl, hard at
work in the broiling sun, pounding cassava in a huge
mortar with a wooden pellett. On remonstrating with
the mistress, who ought to have known better than to
allow it, she excused herself by stating that the girl
was not her's, but the daughter of one of her servants,
who lived on the premises; and on speaking to the latter,
the subject was turned off with such stupid indifference,
as to allow us no room to hope for improvement.
Many of the Haytien mothers appear utterly dead to
all moral considerations, and leave their children to grow
up as they please, the victims of wayward passion, and
of conduct without restraint. The government has provided no schools for boys, except in the larger towns,
and for girls no where. What can be expected from
a people without religion, and without education?
The owner of this property was a mulatto woman of
middle age, apparently uneducated, who entertained a
strong prejudice against the blacks; and lamented that
the President could not be induced to pass a law for
compelling them to work. There is an aristocracy of
the skin, even in Hayti, where all the institutions are
founded on the principle of putting it down. This
springs from the pride and tyranny of the old French

colonists; and it is one of the cruel legacies bequeathed by slavery.

Having eaten a scanty meal, and payed for it handsomely, we rode on to " *La coupe de pentarde*"—the guinea fowl defile—so named from the multitudes of wild guinea fowls that inhabit this part of the island, and afford game to the Haytien sportsmen. At this spot, the view is wide and extensive, and highly interesting. A range of naked chalk hills extends right and left in a curved direction to the sea; embracing a well wooded plain, of about twelve miles in depth, traversed by broad roads leading to Gonaives, St. Mark, and their neighbouring villages. The shipping of Gonaives and the islands of the ocean beyond are visible; and every thing bespeaks a numerous population and an advancing civilization. It was market-day at Gonaives: hundreds of people had passed us within the last two hours; wending their way homeward to the high mountains: the sight surprised us, and seeing other groups in the distance, we began to count the people. Before entering the town itself, we had passed in all four hundred and sixty-five persons, with nearly as many horses, mules, and asses, drawing light carriages, or loaded with commodities, which the peasantry were carrying back, in return for the small parcels of cotton and coffee which they had carried to market. The women, as usual, were decently dressed; and the men were more respectable in appearance than any we had seen on our route: they were evidently small cultivators who live on their own freeholds. All seemed cheerful and happy. It was one of the most cheering sights we saw in Hayti; and we could not but contrast it with those dark and terrible days, when slave proprietors, under the

French dominion, oppressed the people with intolerable hardships; and inflicted cruelties too horrible to relate. In this very region, within the memory of many living witnesses, Deodune, a cotton planter, buried some of his slaves in the earth as deep as their shoulders, and to satisfy his revenge, or for devilish amusement, rolled stones at their heads till they died! The rest of his slaves then rose, and in indignation put the monster himself to death.

So hot was the day, and so wearisome the toil of riding, that we journeyed only at a foot pace: our guide, who had walked with us from Plaisance, his sword girded at his side, tripped nimbly along; performing his part of the journey, about thirty miles, with ease and alacrity, often outstripping us on the road. The last few miles of the plain proved excessively toilsome to us; my wife kept up her spirits tolerably well; but I scarcely knew how to sit my horse; and, what added to our trials, we entered the long town of Gonaives without knowing where we should find a resting-place. No inn or tavern, or public boarding-house to be heard of! We had been told of an English merchant who resided there; to his house, therefore, we made our way, and to our great joy were cordially received as guests by himself, his wife, and daughter. The servant had not yet arrived with the baggage; but our new friends supplied all our need out of their own wardrobe; and after plentiful washings, and an excellent evening meal, we retired to a sumptuous lodging-room to rest.

The next day was the first of the week—the Christian Sabbath. There were only two Protestant families in the place, one of which was that of our hospitable host, James Ostler from Cornwall, who in the morning of that day reads the service of the Church of England in his own parlour. The Roman Catholics had lost their priest, who was gone from home, and there was no one to fill his place. Here, therefore, was a town of 5000 inhabitants, in which no public worship of any kind was performed; except that some of the women, and perhaps a few men, as is common in Catholic countries, entered the parish church to cross themselves with holy water, count their beads, and say their prayers. Several of the respectable inhabitants paid us a visit during the day; to whom, as well as to others before we left, we gave religious books and tracts; which, from the influ- ence they exercise, and from their imposing no money- tax on the people, a woman at the Cape was pleased to designate as " *Les petits predicateurs qui ni mangent ni boivent.*" Among them were publications of the Paris Religious Tract Society ; Lives of pious individuals, Barthe's Annals of the Christian Church and Bunyan's Pilgrim's Progress, all in French ; and a variety of little works to illustrate and to explain the principles of the Society of Friends on Christian doctrine, slavery, and war. Bibles and Testaments were asked for, which I promised to send from Port-au-Prince. Our servant not arriving with the baggage, and notice having reached us that his horse had broken down on the rough road near *Les Escaliers,* twenty miles behind us; we engaged a man and horse to go in quest of him, and direct him to take back the saddle horses we had hired of his master, and to send us the baggage which he held in charge. Late at night, as we were about retiring to rest, the aforesaid servant, to our astonishment, made his appearance; the wicked fellow had refused to de- liver up the baggage to another, on the plea, that he was bound to deliver it with his own hands! He had, therefore, urged on his broken-down steed, and brought back our horses, making a journey to the latter of forty long miles, and bringing them in at an hour of the night when no grass or provender could be procured. Our very hearts sunk within us at the thought of three horses, jaded with toil, exhausted and hungry, condemned to pass a wearisome night without food; and we could not help bitterly reproaching him for his grievous misconduct. He received the reprimand very stupidly : his whole thoughts seemed to be wrapped up in a promise I had made him, that if he brought us safely to Gonaives, I would make him a small present. To gain this trifling douceur, he had ventured to torment three poor dumb animals with a long and painful journey—not feeding them by the way—and to run the risk of starving them for at least ten hours longer. The morning came, and by dint of solicitation, we procured a few bundles of juicy reeds, (no grass could be found) and when the horses had eaten these and drank some water, he turned their heads homeward, and led them away. He deserved nothing but reproof, or to have been led before a magistrate; but I gave him two Haytien dollars and sent, by a private hand, a letter to his master to expose his misconduct. Our host believed that he and his companion had broken down the poor baggage horse by alternately riding him. The circumstance taught me this lesson, which every traveller in Hayti would do well to observe; that is, never to keep in advance of the guide, nor lose sight of your baggage; but always to keep the train before you, however slow you may be compelled to travel.

The town of Gonaives, where we were now located,

is situated at the head of a small bay on the western
shore: the houses are mostly of wood, and of one story;
the streets are long, with a large square in the centre,
on one side of which stands the parish church, now in
ruins. It has a good harbour for shipping, and a noble
convenient quay, where logs of mahogany lie piled up
in great quantities. The exports of the place are
cotton, coffee, mahogany, and salt. The annual exports
of coffee, coastwise and abroad, average about four
millions and a half of pounds' weight annually; those
of cotton, including the district of St. Mark, more than
a million of pounds; and those of mahogany, 800,000
feet. There is, of course, a custom-house, but its officers
are badly paid, and till lately were notorious smugglers.
The chief receives little more than £70 sterling, per
annum. The revenue of Hayti is mainly derived from
duties on articles imported and exported. It was
formerly the common practice of the officers, in concert
with such of the merchants as were willing to enter into
their schemes, to falsify the custom-house returns, and
to enrich themselves at the government expense. No
pains were taken to remedy the abuse, till the honest
merchants, who refused to encourage a contraband commerce, became loud in their complaints: the President
then interfered to put a stop to the evil. The salaries
of the officers, however, owing to the depreciated paper
currency in which they are paid, are still wretchedly
inadequate. The two great shipping ports for mahogany
timber, are Gonaives and Santo Domingo. The mahogany
shipped from this part of Hayti grows on the mountains, about a hundred miles in the interior; in a part of
the island which once belonged to Spain. A merchant
residing at Gonaives, or at the great salt works, (Les

grandes salines,) at the mouth of the Artibonite, goes to
a tract of land where the trees are in maturity; and
bargains with the proprietor for, perhaps, a whole forest,
at a given price per tree. He then has his oxen driven
to the spot, and engages a band of wood-cutters—men
who live in these districts, and devote themselves to
wood-cutting as their only employment. In the last
quarter of the moon the hatchet begins its work; the
forest rings with the sound, and mighty trees fall pros-
trate. The merchant, attended by some workmen, skilful
to discover flaws, or to find out unsound timber, then
perambulates the woods; makes his selection of all the
good trees; has them cleared of the superfluous branches;
and directs their removal : they are then dragged by
thirty or forty oxen to the bed of the nearest mountain
stream, and left for the floods to roll down. This drag-
ging of trees through the forest, and over hill and dale,
is represented as being an extremely arduous, toilsome,
dangerous, and costly work; occasioning immense personal labour, and the loss of much cattle, who are either
bruised or die from exhaustion. The mountain streams
are nearly dry the greater part of the year; but when
swelled with the rains, they become deep and rapid, and
carry down the timber first to *La petite riviere*, and
thence to the Artibonite which flows into the ocean.
On these streams and rivers, dams are constructed at
different places to arrest the timber : there are dwellings
where men reside who form it into rafts, beginning
with a few logs only, and going on increasing their
bulk, till they reach the mouth of the Artibonite;
where they are made into floating rafts of great size,
and towed by sailing vessels to the port of embarkation.
Extraordinary pains are taken to arrest the mahogany

in its downward course; but much of the heaviest and
best timber sinks in the deep rivers; and, with all the
care bestowed at the different stages of its progress, a
large proportion is necessarily lost in its outlet to the sea.
Much of the drift, borne out to the ocean, is recovered
on the coast, or not far from land, and is restored to
the owner on the payment of salvage; but the merchant lays his account with the definitive loss of one
tree in ten. The large sea-rafts are bound together by
strong iron chains; and the vessels that tow them, being
often numerous and crowding all the sail they can carry,
give at the full season an animated appearance to the
bay and harbour.

Our host at Gonaives, who is an extensive mahogany merchant, told us, that when he began his career
he laughed at the mountain people for cutting down
their trees at a particular period of the moon. He
ordered some stout timber to be felled when the moon
was at the full, but soon found reason to repent his
folly; it had not lain long on the ground before it began
to split of its own accord, and at last burst asunder
with a noise that resembled the firing of cannon! However inexplicable to philosophy the fact may be, the
moon has an undoubted and extraordinary influence
both on the animate and inanimate creation. Different
maladies are known to spring from sleeping in the
moonbeams in the tropical regions; and sometimes, to
persons of weakly temperament, from merely travelling
by moonlight. Many well authenticated cases of suffering from this cause were related to us; which served
to confirm the declaration of the Psalmist, that not
only does the sun smite by day, but the moon by night.
As soon as the mahogany rafts are stranded on the

shore, the merchant again examines and marks his timber, rejecting the unsound logs ; the ends of the wood,
which are often inferior, and, which, owing to the high
duty in this country, are not suited to the English
market are cut off, and sent to the United States ;
where such wood is admitted duty free, and where
it is worked up into cheap furniture. The best and
heaviest logs are measured, branded, valued, and shipped
chiefly to London and Liverpool. A whole forest of
mahogany in the high mountains has sometimes been
purchased at a dollar a tree ; the present price of an
extensive cut is about three dollars a tree. Logs are
often selected which readily sell in London for £100
sterling. My friend, James Ostler, shipped one from
Gonaives, that measured 1600 feet, which was sold at
2s. 6½d. per foot, and realized him more than £200.
Millions of lance wood spars, might be exported from
this country ; but they are said to be too heavy to float
on the rivers, and land carriage would be too expensive.
The Haytien government forbids the cutting down of
any timber adapted to ship-building, except for the
ships of Hayti ; and as Hayti has no ships of her own,
but a few brigs and sloops, her large forests of oak and
bayone, del maria, and cancagou woods, (the latter of
which is harder and heavier than mahogany,) are suffered
to go to decay. The palma christi plant grows everywhere in this region, and yields a large quantity of
common castor oil, which sells at two shillings the
gallon. Salt is made in large quantities on the sea-
shore at *Les grandes salines* ; and furnishes a supply for
the whole island. The plains in this neighbourhood
are well adapted to the growth of cotton; the average
price of which in large quantities for shipment is

three-pence sterling per pound. Almost all the cotton
exported from Hayti is grown here; and so numerous
are the small parcels of it which are sent to market from
time to time by the cultivators, that as many as four
thousand horses and asses, laden chiefly with this article,
and with coffee, have been counted at Gonaives in a
single day. In the vicinity of this commercial town are
some banana and plantain groves, belonging to a merchant's family, which we visited much to our gratification.
From the great height of the trees, and from the vast
spreading of their leaves, we could walk at noon-day,
delightfully sheltered from the beams of the sun. A
bunch of plantains or bananas, when the fruit is mature,
is a fine object as it hangs pendant from the upper
branches : this fruit forms part of the staple food of the
country, and seems to be more relished than any other.

Among the few families to whom we were introduced
at this place, was that of the British Vice-Consul,
M'Guffie, a Scotchman by birth, who received us with
much kindness and hospitality. He told us that thirteen
years ago, in 1827 or 1828, twenty-six cases of New
Testaments, French and English in parallel columns,
which had been seized, on the fall of Christophe, by
President Boyer, were sold by auction, at Port-au-Prince,
and bought by a merchant at five cents or two-pence-
halfpenny a copy. These were shipped under the care
of the Vice-Consul himself, to St. Thomas', as part of a
commercial speculation, to be disposed of by De Castra
and Wys; who wondered and laughed at the transaction. Who among all their numerous customers in
the Carribean islands would ever think of asking for
New Testaments ? The Vice-Consul recommended them
to try the market at Martinique, or some other of the

French islands, but never heard afterwards what had
become of them. These books had been sent over, a
long time before, by some philanthropists of England, for
use in the schools of Hayti, and ought not to have been
impounded and sold by the new government. Repeated
applications are said to have been made for the value of
them, but no answer was returned to the applicants.
The public school at Gonaives, during our stay there, was
in abeyance for want of a suitable master; or from the
unwillingness at head-quarters to furnish the needful
salary for his support. Several of the inhabitants complained of the neglect. We left them two sets of
reading lessons for its use when it may be re-opened;
and promised to solicit the authorities at Port-au-Prince
to send them a well-qualified master without delay.
Before taking a final leave of this interesting place, for
such, in some respects, it proved to us, let us for a
moment, revert once again to the memory of Christophe.
Our friend, the British merchant, knew him intimately;
and, as his immediate agent, carried on for him a trade
with Bourdeaux in sugar and coffee; bringing back
French wines, and other commodities and luxuries for
his private consumption. He thought him honourable
in his dealings; but, as a ruler, excessively capricious
and tyrannical. He well remembered the five justices
of Cape Haytien who had given a decision that dis-
pleased the King; and saw them return from the citadel,
where they had been sentenced to hard labour,. in
common working dresses, covered with lime dust. A
man, professing himself to be a prophet, was about the
same time thrown into a lime-kiln and burnt alive; the
King intimating that he must have been an impostor, or
he would have seen his own fate and avoided it!

It was our wish on leaving Gonaives to have proceeded by land, to Port-au-Prince, the capital, a hundred
miles distant; but, independently of the difficulty
of procuring suitable horses and servants, we were
discouraged from taking this step, by learning that the
road, for much of the distance, lay along the naked sea-
shore; that we should pass only through the single town
of St. Mark; and perhaps should be compelled to lodge
one night in the open air, or to put up with the meanest
accommodations in some poor hut, where we should
scarcely find sufficient or proper food. Looking at all
the circumstances, and being told in addition, that the
country was far inferior in picturesque beauty, to that
we had already travelled, we resolved to proceed by sea.
A coasting sloop, loaded with coffee, was ready to sail,
and we took our passage. Our very kind hostess and
her family furnished us with a mattress; and sent on
board for us a liberal supply of cold roasted fowl, eggs,
bread, and bananas. We stipulated for the exclusive
use of the narrow cabin to ourselves.

At ten o'clock, the moon shining bright, we left the
harbour with a good land breeze; and, soon after spreading the mattress on the deck, we lay down to rest, taking
the precaution to cover our faces with the folds of our
cloaks. A fellow-passenger, afraid like ourselves of the
moon-beams, stretched himself in the ship's boat, and
covered his head as well as his body with a blanket.
Early the next morning, we passed the famous salt
works, at the mouth of the Artibonite; and at noon
were off St. Mark, which lay deep in the bay and was
scarcely visible. This town contains 2000 inhabitants,
besides a numerous garrison; and is governed by a
mayor, the only white man, we believe, who holds a

place of authority in the island. We had the pleasure
of making acquaintance with this functionary at the
capital; and learned from himself that he owes this
mark of distinction to the friendship of the President;
who, when an exile in the United States, received
attentions from his father's family. The law of Hayti,
which forbids a white man to hold land, to exercise
authority, to marry a Haytien woman, or to trade
without a special licence, was relaxed in his favour : he
was permitted to marry the daughter of General
Bonnett, the commander of the district, and to exercise
all the rights of a Haytien citizen. No produce is
exported from St. Mark direct to foreign countries ; all
its trade is coastwise. It is said to be a handsome
town, built after the fashion of France, and to be inhabited by some respectable and rather wealthy families.
Dessalines had his palace in the vicinity, and made it
his chief military post. The wind, which was fair at
our setting out, and which we had hoped would have
borne us to Port-au-Prince in twenty-four hours,
changed its course, and blew strongly a-head; we
were, consequently, under the necessity of constantly
tacking, and had the trial and mortification of rolling
three nights on the deep, instead of one. To beat up
against a head wind is painful in any latitude, and in
any craft; but the miseries of a sea-life are, perhaps,
best appreciated by those who, in such circumstances, are confined to a small sloop under the fierce
beams of a vertical sun, without a cabin that can be
used as a shelter, and without canvass for an awning.
The steam from the coffee was so offensive, that we
could not go below deck, and we had only an umbrella
for defence. It was a great mercy to be preserved from

violent sickness; and we were not wholly without
amusement. The coast was interesting to us from its
novelty; and so was the large island of Gonave, and the
islets called the Archadyines; among which we kept
beating up and down for several hours. Necessity
reconciled us to our unpleasant imprisonment. The
wished for port at length came in sight, but our trials
were not yet ended. Our captain was an ignorant man
and had so imperfect a knowledge of his art, that he
twice suffered us to be run upon by a larger vessel entering the harbour under full sail : the first shock was
fearful, and there was much reason to fear we should go
down ; the second was less alarming, but still so serious,
that we were no longer satisfied to remain on board :
the vessel had received injury, and we begged to be
sent on shore in an open boat. We at length arrived
safely at Port-au-Prince, with no other inconvenience
than that of a slight inflammation of the eyes, from the
reflection of a burning sun, and a small degree of sickness, which left us soon after we landed.

CHAPTER V.

THE stranger on first landing at Port-au-Prince, the
capital of Hayti, feels greatly disappointed. Instead of
a handsome city, such as it appears from the ship's
deck at sea, rising on a gradual elevation from the
shore, and adorned with good houses and gardens; you
enter into streets of wooden buildings, with the pavement dislocated or broken up, the drains neglected, and
filth and stable dung interrupting your steps in every
direction. The quay is spacious, but the water is
shallow near the shore; and all sorts of uncleanness are
suffered to annoy the senses. A constant malaria is the
consequence, which at certain seasons of the year,
renders the lower quarter of the city very sickly, and
occasions much mortality among the sailors from foreign
ports. Port-au-Prince, with all its advantages of situation, with every inherent capability of being made and
kept delightfully clean, is perhaps the filthiest capital
in the world. The houses in general are of two
stories, built slightly of wood, to avoid the rend and
tear occasioned by earthquakes, which at different times
have nearly demolished the city. Some few of the
better habitations are of brick or stone, and may be
called handsome edifices. The senate-house is a plain

substantial building, with no pretension to splendour;
and the palace of the President, the largest edifice in the
city, was built by the English, for the General's head-
quarters, during their temporary occupation of the south
of the island; and is, therefore, as little like a royal
palace as any republican could desire. The Haytien flag,
of red and blue, floats on its turrets; and it has in front
a spacious court, in which are lodges for the military
guard of horse and foot, who are constantly on duty.
These are the only public buildings worthy of notice.
The Roman Catholic church is a capacious structure,
but very plain and homely. There are some pleasant
walks and rides in the immediate vicinity, especially in
the hills above the town, and on the roads leading to
Pétionville and Leogane; but none is more generally
agreeable than the extensive park-like fields at the back
of the President's house; where horsemen and pedes-
trians repair every morning and evening to enjoy the
cool breezes, and to watch the rising and setting of the
sun. The public cemetery is a spot of ground which
every stranger should visit; and a funeral procession at
the close of day, winding along the public paths that
lead to it, produces a very striking and solemn effect.
The black boys in their white surplices, bearing lighted
tapers—the massive silver crucifix—the mitred Abbé and
his attendant priests and choristers—the coffin placed
on an open palanquin—and a long train of citizens—
the men habited in black, the women in white—passing
now through the public street, and now in side paths
under the shade of tropical trees, afford a picture which
has no counterpart in our own country. The length of
the city is about a mile; its breadth something less.
The population is estimated at twenty-three thousand.

Numerous ships lie at anchor in the harbour, bearing the flags of different nations; and the bustle of commerce is constantly going on. The custom-house stands on the quay, and is a scene of great activity.

The first call we made in the city after landing was on a French woman, who had formerly kept a boarding house, and to whom we had been recommended for lodgings. She had quitted her profession a few weeks before, and was now living a retired life; but she requested us to enter her house, and refresh ourselves; she readily prepared us breakfast, and directed us where to look for apartments, sending her servant to conduct us, but would take nothing in return. On pressing her to accept some consideration for her pains, she replied with a kind benevolent look, "*Ma religion me commande l'exercice de l'hospitalité. Je ne puis rien prendre: rien de tout.*" We took care, however, to furnish her with a supply of religious books, which she accepted thankfully. We found much difficulty in procuring good accommodations; but succeeded at last in obtaining two large apartments on a ground floor, in one of the principal streets, for the use of which, and board at the public table, we agreed to pay fifty Haytien dollars, or £3. 17s. sterling, per week. We found no cause to regret the arrangement; as by this means we combined private retirement with the advantage of access to good society; and found ourselves in the very focus of news and general information. We had here the occasional company of merchants of the city, planters from the neighbourhood, travellers from distant parts of the country, and Roman Catholic priests, who come to the capital either to consult with the President, who is head of the church, or to see something of the busy world.

The conversation at table was generally carried on in French, but sometimes in English, out of compliment to us ; as we seldom passed a day without meeting with some person who understood the language, and who seemed pleased with the opportunity of speaking it.

Having been furnished with a letter of introduction to the Abbé D'Echeverria, the principal ecclesiastic of Hayti, I waited on him early to present it ; and was received by him with much affability and politeness. He spoke to me of matters connected with the church, and of its temporalities, which he represented as slender enough ! I ventured to remind him that sixty Haytien dollars were allowed by law for a funeral of the first class, and a dollar for every baptism. " These dollars," he said, " are the sweat of our brow," *(le sueur de nos fronts)* " but the government impounds a large part of them, and applies it to other uses ; we only obtain twenty dollars for a funeral, and half a dollar for baptizing an infant. What is half a dollar for a baptism ?" In a day or two after, the Abbé returned my call, and requested us, as friends to the abolition of slavery, to pay him a visit at the presbytery : if we would come and dine with him, we should meet, he said, some of the first people of the city. The banquet, for such it was, greatly exceeded our expectations ; its cost and magnificence were far beyond any idea we had formed of the power of priestly wealth in this country. It carried us back in imagination to the times of Cardinal Wolsey. The company consisted of our generous host —the Abbé himself, the Chief Judge of the Court of Cassation, three senators of Hayti, five merchants of the city, three Roman Catholic priests, a physician, who married the only daughter of General Inginac, with his amiable and intelligent wife, and ourselves. It would be useless to enumerate the various courses and dishes that were served on the occasion. Soups, fish, flesh, fowl, and game were brought on the table and removed in quick succession, together with a great variety of ices, creams, pastry, and comfitures: there was also a splendid dessert and many kinds of wine. As soon as the repast was ended, the Abbé rose and pronounced a eulogium on the virtues of the President; and then, in allusion to his stranger guests, spoke of the efforts made by England to destroy slavery and the slave-trade in all parts of the world. It was his wish, as an old friend of Gregoire and La Fayette, to give these guests a welcome to Hayti, and to introduce them to his fellow-citizens, as deserving of their high respect and kindest attentions. Nothing could be more cordial than his manner, or exceed his polite attention to us all. On retiring to the drawing-room, coffee was immediately served, and some animated conversation followed. We spent a pleasant and instructive evening; and returned home agreeably impressed with the good sense and politeness of the company, who were all coloured persons, except the four priests and ourselves.

The next post of honour and influence to that of the President has long been occupied by General Inginac, a man of colour, who spent some of his early days in Jamaica, and who speaks the English language with great fluency. To him also we had a letter of introduction, as well as one to President Boyer, from th venerable Clarkson. The General received us very courteously, and promised me an early interview with

E

the President. In the meanwhile we pursued our inquiries relative to the state and condition of the people. One of the first objects to claim our attention was the public schools. There are two institutions of this sort in the capital; one on the principle of mutual instruction, for the poor; and the other, a lyceum or college for young men who have received preliminary instruction elsewhere, and who go there to complete their studies. Both schools are supported by the government. In the first, or elementary school, the number of those who attend is very small indeed; out of eighty-two boys on the list, only forty-three were present, and these were most of them mulattos: they looked intelligent enough, but had evidently been neglected, and knew very little; being placed under the care of an incompetent master, who received the situation, and enjoys the slender emolument it affords, because, as we were told, the government thought it convenient to pension him off! We examined the classes, and heard some of the boys recite; but found, on the whole, very little to approve: yet our visit was thought worthy of notice in the Government Gazette, and our approbation of it paraded in a long article written by the master, in order, as we supposed, to commend himself. The lyceum is a really respectable institution, and does honour to the republic. The branches of education taught, are the French, English, Spanish, and Latin languages; the mathematics, composition, history, and fencing. The professors, or teachers, are apparently well qualified men: we attended all the classes, and were much gratified at the progress of some of the scholars. One of the black boys

construed his Latin verses with much readiness. The
students are a hundred and fifty in number, mostly
mulattos : they are attired in a uniform of blue and
scarlet. A public examination takes place at stated
intervals, at which prizes of useful books are given to
those who have made the greatest proficiency. We
went on one of these occasions to witness the proceedings, but came away greatly disappointed. The stage
was first occupied by the young fencers, who came in
armed with a vizor, a blunted sword, and large stuffed
gloves; when numerous encounters took place, to the
amusement and delight of some of the spectators, but to
our disgust, and we speedily retired from the scene.
This practice of training the Haytien youth to the art of
fencing has a most prejudicial effect on the community :
the practice of duelling, already dreadfully rife in the
island, is strengthened by it, and a warlike spirit engen-
dered and fostered, which it should be the particular
and earnest aim of the government to discourage and put
down. What has Hayti, or what is it likely to have, to
do with foreign war? Peace is the safety of the Haytien
people; peace should be the end and object of all her
institutions. To teach fencing systematically in her
public schools, is to encourage an art that may one day
be turned against the republic itself, and plunge the
country into civil war. The sword which is now used
as a plaything, may soon be stained with the blood of
citizens.

Education is at a rather lower ebb at Port-au-Prince
than at Cape Haytien : the total number supposed to
receive instruction in the city is about a thousand, as
follows :—

E 2

Boys at the school for mutual instruction   80
At the Lyceum   .   .   . 150
At fifteen private pedagogue schools   . 450
Girls at eight seminaries and dame schools 200
Boys and girls taught at home   .   120
                                        ─────
                    Total   .   1000

This number is small, but the proportion of black children, unhappily, is still smaller. Out of 23,000 inhabitants, the coloured class may number, perhaps, 4000, or one-sixth part of the whole; yet this is the class that may be said to monopolise education. Children who claim their descent from European fathers have no greater aptitude to learn than children of pure African blood; but the ancestors of the latter having been slaves, and not having been taught to read, were unable to appreciate the value of education. Indifference to know-ledge, from this cause, has extended from one generation to another, and has become a rooted habit of mind; which requires the most firm, judicious, and persevering care to eradicate. The subject of education in Hayti is well worthy the attention of philanthropists. Schools must be established, maintained and multiplied in the island, or it will never recover itself from the dominion of semi-heathenism, superstition, and priestcraft, by which its people are still fettered, or be likely to put forth that industry which will increase the fruits of the soil, and enable it, as an agricultural and commercial country, to take rank among civilized nations. If the government of Hayti, stimulated by precept, and assisted by the efforts of the friends of education in England, be determined to exert itself to spread light and knowledge, the fatal lethargy of the black people

will soon be shaken off. With ample means to educate
their children, they only want the disposition : the
priests, who, too generally " love darkness rather than
light," may for a time oppose the movement, but every
difficulty may be overcome by perseverance.

In a population so circumstanced, where all the nobler
faculties of the mind are held in abeyance, we need not
wonder if crime abounded. Ignorance is proverbially
the parent of crime : yet such is the docility of the
negro, such his respect for, and general submission to,
the authority of human law, that robberies of the
person, and other high crimes and misdemeanours, are
but little known. Petty pilfering, such as the masters
of slaves once permitted, and such as the boasting
Spartans encouraged, is common enough; and it is
from offences of this sort and from acts of military
insubordination, that the gaols are kept constantly
filled. We were assured again and again by persons
of every rank in society, that travellers may pass
through the country from one end to the other, with
known treasure in their possession, and be perfectly
safe. The military ·institutions, as we shall presently
see, encourage and confirm the practice of petty thieving,
and have given rise to many, if not most, of the vices
that prevail. We requested leave to visit the city-
prison, of the Adjutant-commander of the district, who
deferred giving us an answer; but on the next morning one of the President's aides-de-camps came to our
lodging with a written permission. The gaoler, who
had been apprised of our coming, entered with alacrity,
and with much shew of consequence, on his duty.' Two
officers with drawn swords attended him, and ourselves,
through the apartments. A young man, who acted as

secretary, followed with pen, ink, and paper, and noted down the observations we made in passing along; which observations were all read over to us, to be verified and attested, before we left. The prison has three courts, of about an equal size, fifty-four feet by twenty seven. The court, No. 1, contains four apartments, and had in it, at the time of our visit, twenty-one prisoners. The court, No. 2, has eight apartments, and consequently less airing room, but contained eighty-one prisoners! The court, No. 3, was devoted to the military, and had in it thirty-one soldiers, who occupied four apartments, and were confined for breaches of military discipline. There is also one other court, No. 4, larger than the foregoing, with one large room, and several small ones, in which men and women are confined for petty offences for a short period only : the yard and apartments being open in the day time to both sexes without restraint, and with little or no inspection! All the rooms of the prisons were clean and well white-washed. There is a fountain of water within the walls, which affords a ready and inexhaustible supply. The faults of this prison are too numerous to mention : the chief defects are want of ventilation, want of space for exercise, and want of classification. The prisoners are thus enumerated :—*Prévenus*, sent by the Commandant and other public officers, for petty offences; and prisoners not yet tried ; 95. *Travaux forcés*, convicts sentenced to hard labour and the chain gang ; 29. *Femmes accusés et condamnées*, women convicts ; 14. *Condamnées aux correctionels*, sentenced to be whipped ; 8. *A la reclusion*, to occasional solitary confinement ; 9. Lunatiques, Insane ; 6. Total, exclusive of the military ; 161.

One-quarter of a Haytien dollar (five-pence sterling)

is allowed weekly to each prisoner to purchase food; what he requires of food more than this, he must work for, or his friends, if he has any, must supply. A physician is appointed to visit the sick, and to prescribe food and medicine for them, according to their wants. No prisoner, we were told, really suffers from hunger; but this statement was contradicted by so many persons out of doors, that we doubt the fact. Many cases of starvation are believed to have occurred; and it is certain that the prisoners often quarrel and contend with each other for the orange and banana peelings, which those who have sufficient food are contented to throw away. The common work of the prisoners is to make mats and baskets. Some of the men are nearly naked. Such is a brief view of this wretched place of confinement; which, if it reform one convict through terror, is calculated to harden twenty, and to turn them loose on society, to begin a fresh career of vice. Let not Englishmen, however, reproach the African race as barbarous, for permitting such prisons to exist; the gaols of England, half-a-century ago, were many of them equally wretched.

If the prisons of Hayti be bad, the criminal jurisprudence is no better; and stands in equal need of a thorough reformation. The officers of the army act in many cases as justices; and pass sentence for petty offences, on summary conviction. What a wide field for abuse is here! The sentences passed by the civil judges in open court, though seemingly the result of deliberation after a patient trial of the parties accused, are said, in all cases thought worthy of government interference, to be prescribed beforehand. That such is sometimes the case is certain; for a grave in the unconsecrated

burial ground was pointed out to us, which was opened
for three criminals charged with sedition, before they
had been put on trial!

Accompanied by my friend, James Hartwell, the
Wesleyan missionary, who had been with us through
the prison, I entered the Court-house to witness the trial
of a prisoner accused of stealing cloth from a store.
The *procureur-general*, or state-attorney opened the
case. Rising with all the dignity of an important
public functionary, he put on his official hat, and
addressing himself to the judges on the bench, two
of whom sat covered, he vehemently urged his proofs
of the prisoner's guilt; he then called his witnesses,
but none appeared. The attorney for the prisoner
then rose, and contended that as there was no evidence
adduced, he was entitled to an immediate acquittal.
The state-attorney again rose, bowed to the bench,
put on his hat as before, and urged in reply, that inasmuch as the crime had been distinctly proved before
a magistrate appointed to take the examination, *in
limine*, and this examination was on record before the
court, and nothing was now advanced by the prisoner
to establish his innocence, the absence of witnesses was
immaterial, and he must by law be pronounced guilty.
The court, consisting of two mulattos and an intelligent
looking black man, then retired, and were gone about
half-an-hour. During their absence, the two attorneys,
accuser and defender, came to my friend and myself,
and asked us what, in such a case, would be the
verdict of an English jury. We had no difficulty in
saying, that he would be acquitted without a moment's
hesitation. Whilst we sat waiting the return of the
judges with their verdict of acquittal, the side door

opened, and a herald came forward, and proclaimed
attention; then the chairman read deliberately the
prisoner's sentence, that he was condemned to three
years' labour in the chain-gang! Immediately, conducted by two soldiers with fixed bayonets, and wearing
a look of consternation and dismay, he was led out of
court to his prison-house. Incidents such as these, and
others that we met with, were often the subjects of conversation at the dinner-table, and elicited comments
from the company that put us in possession of the state
of public feeling with regard to these matters. The
intelligent part of the Haytien people are evidently at
variance with their own government on many public
points,—and especially as regards the administration of
justice.

Our conversation at dinner sometimes turned on
slavery and freedom. On one occasion, several planters,
three of them brothers, from a sugar property in the *Cul
de Sac*, were present. The eldest, who had been educated
in Paris, addressing the company, said, "Nous avons
parmi nous un Negrophile; voulez vous que nous buvions
a sa santé;" and turning to me, "Voulez vous nous
permettre a boire a votre santé?" The custom of
drinking healths is not so common in Hayti as in
England; and it may be hoped is going out of fashion
everywhere. Without joining in the senseless ceremony, I left them to do as they pleased, but took care
from the circumstance, to turn the discourse into a
channel which elicited from the company some striking
remarks, condemnatory of those nations which permit
slavery to continue.

All classes of Haytien citizens, old and young, rich
and poor, are loud in their denunciations of slavery and

E 3

the slave-trade : they dislike the Americans, on account
of their permitting slavery to exist, but receive Englishmen with complacency, because the latter have done so
much to put an end to the horrid system. The mayor
of St. Mark was often at our table ; with whom
we held conversations on the state of education in
his own district, and whom we furnished with some
sets of school lessons, which he promised to see appro-
priated to their intended use. A Lancasterian school
for boys, founded by Christophe, still exists in his
municipality.

Among the inhabitants of Port-au-Prince, who showed
us kindness and hospitality, we are bound to mention
one English merchant who has much influence in the
city, and who acts as Consul for the kingdom of Sweden.
From him and from his amiable wife we received the
kindest attentions ; which, as being strangers in a
foreign land, were peculiarly grateful to us. At his
dinner-table we met on one occasion, together with
other visitors, the British Consul-General, who was
about to return home ; the Vice-Consul of Port-au-
Prince ; and the Consul from Cape Haytien. The
conversation turned chiefly on war, which most of
the company joined in approving, as one great means
of elevating the power of England, and making her
respected among the nations ! Our war with China
seemed to meet with especial favour ; but for what moral
reason it was not easy to comprehend. Much was said
by the company, and no doubt with great truth, of the
covetousness, lying and gambling of many of the Romish
priests, who come from France and Corsica to this island
as money adventurers ; not to help the needy and in-
struct the ignorant ; but to make, from the superstitions

of the common people, as much money as possible in the shortest possible time.

Having called a second time on General Inginac, he obligingly gave me an introduction to General Boyer, the President. An aid-de-camp in waiting led me to the hall of audience; and in a few minutes after, the President himself, attired in a plain suit of black, entered by a private door, and taking me by the hand, requested me to follow him to his own apartment. The manners of the ruler of Hayti are simple and unaffected; to republican plainness, he adds the polish of France, and preserves a quiet independent dignity suited to his rank and station. His age is sixty-eight; but his robust health and evident activity, make him appear much younger. He is a mulatto, with the physiognomy of the French; is rather under than over the average height; and is neither thin nor corpulent: he has a keen expressive eye, and an intelligent countenance. With strangers he converses only in French; though he has travelled in America, and understands the English language. During the interview of half an hour, with which he kindly favoured me, he made particular inquiries after the venerable Clarkson; with whose character, as a strenuous advocate of the abolition of slavery and the slave-trade, he was well acquainted; and of whom he had a more intimate knowledge than of other men, from his correspondence with Christophe, in which he manifested such an intense interest in the best welfare of Hayti. "All the letters of Wilberforce and Clarkson, addressed to Monsieur Christophe," such were his words, "are in my possession: they thought highly of the man, but they did not understand his real character: they thought him the genuine friend of his country, but he deceived them." " I received a letter from Mr. Clarkson," he continued, " soon after the death of Christophe, in which he requested me to show kindness to his widow. I thought it somewhat singular; for though Christophe was a cruel man, and though he killed my own brother, I would have forfeited my life a thousand times, rather than have shown unkindness to his widow. I always protected Madame Christophe." " He entertained," he said, " a high regard for the religious Society of Friends : he had known some of that body in America, and was acquainted with some of their customs. I might depend on his protection whilst in Hayti ; and he had given an order to the authorities to furnish me with all the papers I had asked for, to illustrate the resources and condition of the republic." He wished me however, as a stranger, not to overlook the single fact, that Hayti was a young nation : that it was only yesterday, that she was released from the menaces and fears of France, by a new treaty of compensation for her ter- ritory ; and that till the present time there had been no opportunity for the government to devote itself in earnest on peace-principles, to improve the institutions of the country. On rising to take leave, I begged per- mission to present him with some religious publications, handsomely bound : he received them very courteously ; and on observing a series of the tracts of the Peace Society, which had been translated into the French language, he said with an air and tone of sincerity, " If the principles of that Society had been acted upon by the nations, what an accumulation of misery would the world have been spared !"

The papers alluded to by the President, were soon

after put into my hands by General Inginac, his
Secretary of State; and these enable me, in conjunction
with information obtained from other quarters, to lay
before the reader a brief statement of the commerce,
finances, and expenditure of the island, the number
and pay of the standing army, and the employments
and resources of the agricultural population.   To these
I may add, some information on the constitution of
Hayti, in church and state; and some observations on
the estimated amount of its population.

CHAPTER VI.

CONSTITUTION OF HAYTI—CHURCH ESTABLISHMENT—
ARMY—COMMERCE—FINANCE — EMPLOYMENTS AND
CONDITION OF THE PEOPLE — ESTIMATE OF THE
POPULATION.

THE constitution of Haytí, as now embodied in the
statutes of the island, was finally modified in 1816. The
government of the republic is confided to a President,
chosen for life, who has power to nominate his successor
at death, reserving to the senate the right, if they see fit,
to reject the nomination, and choose any other citizen
they may prefer. The legislative power is vested in three
branches, which must all concur in passing the laws:
1st, The President, with whom all the laws originate:
2nd, The Senate, chosen for nine years, who are selected
from lists presented by the President to the House
of Assembly for its choice: 3rd, The House of Representatives, chosen for five years by free election of the
people assembled in their respective communes; who
are professedly and in theory, an independent body, at
liberty to call in question the management of public
affairs, and to address the President on any occasion, as
often as they will. The salary of the President is 40,000
Haytien dollars per annum, with an extra salary of
30,000 dollars when engaged in any one year in travelling through the island on a tour of inspection for the
public good. Each Senator has a salary paid by the

State of 133 dollars per month; and each Representative
receives 200 dollars per month during the session of
Congress. The Haytien dollar at the present rate of
exchange is one shilling and eight pence. The salary
of the President, therefore, in sterling money is £3333;
and, when travelling, £2500 per annum in addition:
the salary of a Senator is £133 per annum; and that of
a Representative to the House of Assembly, during a
session of three months, about £50. The constitution,
however liberal it may appear in theory, and containing,
as it does, some of the essential elements of a republic,
is, in practice, often at variance with the liberties and
true happiness of the people. The President is chosen
for life: he takes care in presenting lists to the House
of Representatives, for the choice of Senators, so to
arrange the names, as to ensure the election of the
persons that he wishes; and from the comparative
poverty and ignorance of many members of the House
of Assembly, who are always subservient, he can
influence the decision of that body at his pleasure; even
so far as to induce them to expel any member who
manifests the least show of resistance to his will. The
President of Hayti, being governor for life, generalissimo
of the forces, head of the church, and fountain of honour
and rewards, is thus a sovereign in all but the name.
The maxims of his government are those of clemency,
and to rule for the people's good; but a mistaken view
of what that good really requires, leads him occasionally
into acts of substantial injustice. The constitution prescribes that a law should be passed to regulate the choice
of soldiers for the army: no project of such a law has yet
been presented, and the citizens are called out, impressed,
and compelled to serve in the ranks at the will of the

executive. Many and bitter are the complaints on this
head, especially from the merchants and traders, who see
their sons sometimes torn from them, to be placed side by
side with ragamuffins, who are satisfied with the parade
and idleness of a military life; and who, from long continuance in it, have become as demoralized and corrupt,
as the profession of arms can make them. Do the citizens
who feel this oppression look to their representatives for
help ? They know that all appeal of this sort would be
useless. Only four years ago, early in 1838, in consequence of a bold address to the President, a strife was
stirred up between the two Houses of the Legislature;
and the House of Representatives was prevailed upon
by a majority, to expel six of its best and most honest
members ! It is impossible to read the printed proceedings and votes of this little parliament, without at
once seeing on which side the wrong lies. The following
sensible and spirited remarks contained in the address,
occasioned the disturbance. But what shall we say of
the subserviency of a legislative body that adopted such
a resolution by acclamation one month, and pronounced a
vote of expulsion on its supporters the next ? " Le choc
qui existe entre les principes fondamentaux et les dispositions reglementaires de la constitution sont une antinomie
qui doit disparaitre du code des droits et des devoirs.
L'expérience proclame cette verité : les dispositions
reglementaires d'une constitution arretent le jeu libre des
ressorts du gouvernement, dont les principes fondamentaux sont le mobile : elles amoindrissent la somme de
bien qui doit devoiler de son action. La nation vous sup-
plie donc d'assurer son avenir : vous en avez la puissance
et le genie : aujourd'hui que la paix est imperturbable,
il n'est plus tems d'ajourner. Exprimez un voeu ; et

bientot des mains régéneratrices reconstruiront l'edifice
social : ravivez nos institutions qui sont deja menacés
de vetusté, parcequ' aux yeux du pays, elles sont
insuffisantes pour les besoins de la societé." * The
house then goes on to request from the President the
projects of new laws suited to the exigency of the
times, among which are enumerated, a law to insure
the responsibility of public functionaries—to alter the
custom-house duties—to fix the rate of interest and
repress usury—to restrict the power now given to
Justices of the Peace—to determine suits on summary
conviction without appeal ; and a law to modify the
severities of the *Code Rural*, which it denounces as at
variance with public feeling, and therefore inoperative
to its end. " Si nous examinons à present l'instabilité
de certaines lois, nous nous etonnerions de les voir
s'arreter tout a coup, comme frappées d'inertie, après
avoir pris un essor rapide ; de ce nombre, on distingue
le code rural. Il est tombé, et sa chute a écrasé
l'agriculture ; mais il faut le dire, il a subi le sort de
toutes les institutions qui ne sont pas dans l'esprit du
siecle de perfectionnement. Privé de la sanction de

---

* The clashing of fundamental principles with the details of
the constitution, is a contradiction which must disappear from the
code of rights and duties. Experience proclaims this truth : the
details of a constitution interfere with the free exercise of the
powers of government which should always be regulated by
fundamental principles. They lessen the sum total of the good
which ought to result from its action. The nation entreats you
then to give it security for the future : you have the power and
the genius to do so. At present, peace is undisturbed and secure,
it is therefore no time for delay. Express but the wish, and
regenerating hands will re-construct the social edifice ; re-animate
our institutions which are already threatened with decay, because
in the eyes of the country they are insufficient for the wants of
society.

l'opinion, l'interet même nà pu là garantir dúne desuetude native, mais nous croyons pouvoir avancer, sans
craindre d'etre contredit, que ce code modifié et appro-
prié aux besoins de l'epoque présente, produira les
plus heureux effets."* A few such legislators as these
of Hayti, who write and speak in this spirit, might
be useful in our own House of Commons; but their
reforming hand has been paralysed: the President
thought them too much in advance of the age, and as
requiring more than the public good, or the people at
large could bear! He therefore caused the Assembly
to be decimated, and made their own votes the executioner of his secret decree. The government of Hayti
is in fact a military despotism in the hands of a
single man; mild and merciful it must be confessed,
and desiring the welfare of his country; but mistaken
in some of his views, and therefore acting on some
occasions in a manner utterly opposed to the public
good.

Often did we hear from intelligent Haytiens, serious
complaints of this tendency in the executive; and often
was the wish expressed to us, that the public press
of England and France, might be induced to set forth
their national grievances to the world. " If you publish

---

* If we examine, at the present moment, the instability of
certain laws, we shall be astonished to see them stopped suddenly,
as if struck with *inertia*, after having taken a rapid stride. Of
this number is the rural code. It has fallen, and its fall has
crushed agriculture ; although, it must be confessed it has only
experienced the fate of all institutions that are opposed to the
spirit of an improving age. Deprived of the support of public
opinion, interest itself cannot keep it from falling into desuetude ;
but we think we may assert without fear of contradiction, that
this very code, if so modified as to meet the wants of the present
age, would produce the happiest results.

observations on Hayti," said several of the merchants
and planters to me, "represent us as we are; do not
flatter us; exhibit our true condition; we seek amelioration not by force of arms—we have had bloodshed
and strife enough,—but through the important and
powerful medium of the opinion of observing foreigners,
who see our condition, and can state what it really is."
My object in these pages is to exhibit Hayti and its
institutions as they really are.

Let me now speak of the standing army. The last
account in detail placed in my hands by the government, gives the following enumeration :—Under the
head *Military Appointments*, as commanders of districts,
there are nine generals; fifteen brigadier-generals;
sixty-three colonels; forty-eight lieutenant-colonels;
nine captains; one lieutenant; and twenty medical
men; whose united pay amounted to 188,407 dollars,
or £15,700 sterling. This, in the present depreciated
currency of the island, yields less, on an average, than
£100 sterling to each individual. The pay of a general,
is £225 per annum; that of a brigadier-general, £170;
that of a colonel, £125; that of a lieutenant-colonel,
£66; that of a captain, £25; and that of a lieutenant,
£18.*

The standing army, consists,in addition, of 33 colonels;
95 lieutenant-colonels; 825 captains; 654 lieutenants;
577 sub-lieutenants and ensigns; 6815 non-commissioned
officers; 25 medical men; and 19,127 rank and file :—
total 28,151. The pay of a common soldier is three
dollars per month, or £3. sterling per annum, for one
week on duty out of every three; being at the rate of

---

* The above-mentioned officers are invested with civil as well
as military power.

three shillings and sixpence per week, for every week
that such soldier musters on parade. The total cost of
the army in 1838, including the Arsenals, Hospitals,
and Marines, was in Haytien dollars 1,418,557; or
£118,213 in sterling money : a small sum for the
maintenance of such an immense standing army; but a
much larger sum than Hayti, with her very limited
resources, can afford to pay, or is likely long, to
sustain. The army is in a state of gradual reduction :
its numerical force in 1840, was twenty-five thousand.

By the present arrangements, the common soldier
attends one week on duty in the muster field, and is
left at liberty to go to his own home, or to procure work
where he can the two succeeding weeks; and this reduces
the army *in point of pay*, to one-third of its present
numerical amount; or to 8500 men. An immense army
this, being at the rate of one in a hundred of the whole
population ; whereas, Great Britain and Ireland, war-
loving countries, have but one soldier on pay to every
two hundred and twenty-five of its people ; and many
of the European states, have a smaller proportion still.
Most of the common soldiers of Hayti are, or might be,
cultivators of the soil in their own right, or they might
work on the plantations as sharers of the produce with
the large proprietors. If set entirely free from a military
life, this would be their immediate and natural condition
in society : they would at once return to their native
cabins, and give their strength to the cultivation of
the soil. But the habits of the camp and the barracks
unsettle them ; they are bound to be present at parade,
except under special exemption, once in the week at
all times; and some of them live ten, twenty, and
even thirty miles distant from the muster-ground.

How can men, under such circumstances, devote much
of their two weeks of liberty to agriculture? Six clear
days in a week, every two weeks out of three are their
own ; and of the twelve so allowed, two, three, and
sometimes four days are consumed in going and returning. Thus harassed by marching, when they get no
pay, they become discouraged, grow listless and idle,
and instead of attempting to go home, seek casual
employment near the place of rendezvous ; and, if no
honest profitable labour is at hand, rather than starve,
they will sometimes go to the nearest provision grounds
and help themselves. The small cultivators become
dissatisfied at the frequent robbery of their gardens and
grounds ; and lose much time in hunting out the offenders
and in bringing them to summary justice ; society gets
disorganised ; and all this dreadful inconvenience and
loss, with peril to the morals of the community, is
encountered, that the government may make a display
of a large disposable military force, and be ready
to resist an invasion, which no power, European or
American, has the slightest desire to undertake, or the
hardihood to instigate ! Hayti might safely dismiss her
army altogether ; for she has no enemies abroad to serve
as a pretence for maintaining it ; or, if she need an active
police, let her retain one-fourth of the present soldiers
as policemen, give them a peace uniform, and pay them
good wages. This would be one means, and a very
important one, of regenerating the country. The active
limbs of eighteen thousand strong men, might thus be
employed on the soil, and raise food for the supply of at
least ten times their own number. Look at the pay of
a soldier on duty ; sixpence sterling a day ; scarcely
sufficient to buy the common provisions of life ! What

a wretched system, and how short-sighted the government that permits it to continue. The troops are well accoutred, and pretty well dressed: and the officers, chiefly black men, having no qualification by education for civil service in the state, are ambitious of command in the army. These men must be propitiated and kept in action and pay; and hence in part the continuance of the evil. Besides the standing army above enumerated, there is a militia force in the island of 40,000 men; who assemble one day in every quarter for inspection and a review. Sixty-five thousand soldiers, out of less than a million of people, or one in fifteen of all the inhabitants! Does the House of Representatives ask for reform without cause? Let us now dismiss the army, and take a glance at the church.

The history of the church in Hayti may be given in a few words. At a former period, when the Spanish part of the island was subject to France, the Archbishop of Santo Domingo exercised under the Pope, ecclesiastical supremacy. Since the union of both divisions of the island under the republic, the jurisdiction of the Pope at Rome has been repudiated; the Archbishop has banished himself to a distant country, and the President, following the example of Henry the Eighth, has become head of the church. The religion recognised by law is Roman Catholic; but there is only one order of priests; no archbishops, bishops, deans or other titled dignitaries swell the ecclesiastical muster-roll, or levy contributions on the people. Entire toleration is the law of the land, and is freely extended to all dissentients from the Romish church. There are no tithes for the maintenance of a priesthood, and no forced contributions

for the support of public worship or the repair of
the parish church. Every contribution on the score
of religion is paid for some presumed spiritual benefit,
and the amount to be demanded for each separate
service is regulated by law. The following are the
payments prescribed for church service, by a late act
of the legislature 1840, cap. iv. art. 28. " There shall
be received for a baptism half a dollar. For a marriage, with the performance of mass, eight dollars. For
a marriage without the mass, four dollars. For a mass
thirty-seven cents and-a-half. For a high mass, a
service, or a funeral of the first class, in parishes where
there are churchwardens appointed, sixty dollars ; and in
parishes where there are none, forty dollars. For funerals
of the second class, twenty dollars. For funerals of the
third class, ten dollars. Art. 29. At masses, services,
and funerals of the first class, there shall be in attendance four singers, twelve choristers, a cross-bearer,
sacristan, and swiss, (sacristaine et suisse.) At funerals
of the second class, two singers, six choristers, a
cross-bearer, and sacristan. At funerals of the third
class, one singer, two choristers, a cross bearer, and
sacristan. Art. 30. At services and funerals of the
first class, there shall be a general ringing of bells, a
suite of hangings for the interior and doors of the
church, church-plate complete, with mortuary cloth and
ornaments at the altar. At funerals of the second class, the
ringing of two bells, drapery half way down the church,
mortuary cloth at the altar, and a portion of church
plate. At funerals of the third class, the sounding of a
single bell, mortuary cloth, a smaller portion of plate,
and twelve candles. There shall be also, at funerals of
the first class, hangings at the doors of the residence of

the deceased. Art. 31. At services and funerals of the first class and second class, the necessary tapers are to be furnished by the party who requires the service or funeral. At those of the third class, the church shall furnish them. After the ceremonies, the tapers and candles that remain shall go one-half to the repair of the church, the other half to the priest. Neither rectors nor vicars shall receive any thing for offices at which they do not assist in person, except in cases of sickness."

Such are the fees by which the Romish church in Hayti is sustained. One portion of them is given by law to the churchwardens for the needful repairs of the parish church, and some other parish purposes; or to the council of notable men, where there is a corporation; and the remainder in different defined proportions is bestowed on the rectors, vicars, singers, choristers, cross-bearer, and other officers. Every one by law is paid for what he does, and no one is paid for what he does not. These payments to the church are in one sense a tax, because they are prescribed by law; but they are a tax which any individual who has a conscientious objection to them, may avoid paying, by declining the use of the pre-scribed rites. A mother brings her child to be baptized by the priest, and receives his blessing, and pays half-a-dollar for the presumed benefit; but if she decline the ceremony altogether, or take her child to a protestant missionary for baptism, *the state exacts nothing.* A person dies : the relations of the deceased desire a grand funeral, and pay sixty dollars for the service, sixty dollars for high mass, and sixty for the interment; and receive in return a loud noise of bells, a full choir, and the display of a huge silver crucifix; all this is perfectly intelligible, and looking at religion as a trade or a

plaything is perfectly just; but if the relations or
friends of a deceased person choose to bury the body
in the public cemetery without the intervention of a
priest, the grave is opened to receive it, and *the state
exacts nothing*. A large number of those who die in
remote country places, to save the payment of fees, are
buried without priestly rites or assistance; and many
are buried with the rites of heathenism, such as are
practised to this day in the heart of Africa; but when
poor people die in a town or city, and are buried without the crucifix, because their friends are unable or
unwilling to pay for it, the sympathies of their neighbours are excited towards the memory of the dead, and
reproaches are cast on the church for its covetousness.
The common people, speaking generally, are not very
solicitous to have their deceased relatives buried by the
priest. Water-baptism is thought to be essential to
salvation, and must be performed at all hazards, and
at whatever cost. A registration is made of births and
burials; the recorded number of births may be presumed
to be nearly correct, but no dependence whatever can
be placed on the record of burials as a proof of the
actual mortality. It is impossible to ascertain the
amount of money levied by ecclesiastical charges on the
whole people, as the sums received are not accounted
for to the public treasury. Unless, therefore, access be
obtained to the parish books, there are no means of
arriving at the truth. Approximation to it, is all that can
be looked for. The income of the Abbé D'Echeverria,
at Port-au-Prince, was variously estimated at from
10,000 to 40,000 dollars, or from £800 to £3200 per
annum. Ecclesiastical fees, however, must necessarily
be large in a populous town or parish, where many of

F

the inhabitants, are not of the poorest class; and hence some of the priests become speedily rich. The chief object of the ecclesiastics in Hayti (their number is about seventy) is to secure gold and silver as quickly as they can, to send to Europe for investment: three instances of this sort came under our own observation; in one of which a priest having heard that we possessed some doubloons, came privately to us to bargain for a few of them, to send abroad; and in the others, money to a considerable amount had been placed in the hands of English merchants of our acquaintance to invest in the English and French funds. One priest told me how much he had placed in our Three per cent Consols, and asked me confidentially what I thought of the safety of entrusting his money to a certain merchant in one of the trading towns, for transmission abroad. The means of acquiring wealth, by greedy ecclesiastics, are unhappily always ready to their hand: they encourage superstitious feelings in the people, and receive donatives without law as well as by virtue of it. Not contented with baptising children for gain, they baptise houses, boats, and door-posts! A merchant at Gonaives assured us, that he had paid on one occasion twenty dollars to a priest for baptising a small vessel when ready for sea, which belonged to a female friend of his; and related to us many other instances of church rapacity. So mercenary, indeed, have the Romish priests become—many of them are low-bred Corsicans, notorious for habits of debauchery — that General Inginac, in an address to his fellow-citizens, recently published, bestows on them the following indignant and well-merited rebuke :—" Les ecclesiastiques sont sans doute ceux qui par leur état, sont appelés spécialement à travailler sans relàche, soit à l'autel, soit

en particulier, non seulement à prêcher les doctrines de
l'Education Morale et Religieuse, mais encore à en offrir
à chaque instant les exemples qui peuvent le mieux en
faire comprendre l'importance. Or, est-ce bien ce dont
ils s'occupent toujours? Se montrent-ils, tous ceux qui
sont admis à officier dans la République, uniquement
occupés à pénétrer le cœur et l'esprit de leurs ouailles de
ces sentimens sublimes qui vivifient la conscience et
excitent à la pratique des vertus chrétiennes? On
pourrait reprocher à bien des Curés des paroisses d'être
loin de mettre dans l'accomplissement de leurs devoirs
sacrés toute l'onction et l'exactitude que l'on est fondé à
attendre de ceux qui parlent au nom de la Divinité.
Que de grands malheurs ne doivent pas résulter de
l'exemple donné par les Prêtres qui, sans respect pour
ceux qu'on a confiés à leur direction pastorale, *se livrent
à des scandales de tous les genres, qui trahissent et le
Gouvernement paternel qui les protège et le Tout-Puis-
sant dont ils sont les Ministres;* les Prêtres sont des
hommes et ils peuvent faillir lorsque la vertu ne s'est
pas tout-à-fait emparée de leurs âmes et lorsque, n'étant
pas contenus pas une stricte surveillance dans les principes de la saine moralité, et se trouvant au milieu d'un
peuple bon et généreux, *ils ne songent qu'aux avantages
matériels de leurs positions,* sans se préoccuper de l'essen-
tiel de leurs devoirs. Lorsqu'il arrive que des Prêtres se
montrent ainsi infidèles aux obligations qui leur sont
imposées et *qu'ils ne se livrent qu'à l'immoralité ou à
des pratiques superstitieuses, pour mieux en imposer aux
crédules qui s'approchent des autels,* qui doit les rappeler
a leurs pieuses obligations?"*

* The ecclesiastics are, without doubt, the individuals who, from
their station in society, are peculiarly called upon to labour inces-

If the above charges be true, and no one who is acquainted with the state of the country can for a moment doubt, that, they are so; we may use the words of our own Christian poet, and applying them to such a priesthood, say :—

> " A few there are with Eli's spirit blest ;
> Hophni and Phineas may describe the rest."

Dr. England, the Roman Catholic Bishop of Charleston, United States, came out to Hayti, about eight years ago, as the Pope's legate, to try and establish the Pope's supremacy. He found the island in a shocking state. Two of the priests in the presbytery of Port-au-Prince had been galley slaves released from bondage ! The

santly, whether at the altar, or in private life, not only to preach morality and religion, but to offer in their own conduct those exemplifications of doctrine which may the better enable others to comprehend its importance. But is it in this manner that they occupy their time? Do they shew themselves—all those who are admitted to officiate in the republic—solely occupied in endeavouring to penetrate the heart and understanding of their flocks with those exalted sentiments which quicken the conscience, and excite to the practice of Christian virtues ? We may reproach many of the parish clergy with being far from carrying into the performance of their sacred duties, all the unction and the accuracy which we have a right to look for in those who speak in the name of the divinity. What dreadful evils must needs result from the example thus set by the priests, who without regard to those who are confided to their pastoral guidance, give themselves over to all sorts of abominations: who betray both the paternal government which affords them its protection, and the Almighty, whose ministers they are. The priests are men, and must needs fail since virtue has not taken possession of their minds. Not being kept by strict watchfulness in the principles of sound morality, and finding themselves in the midst of a confiding and generous people, they dream only of their own secular advantage, to the entire neglect of their essential duties. Since it happens that the priests are so faithless to their obligations, devoting themselves only to immorality, and to superstitious practices, that they may the more readily impose on the credulous, who approach the altars; who, we may ask, should recall them to a sense of their religious duties?

immorality and debauchery of others had become so
notorious that the Council of Notables took up the
matter; and when the priests refused, as *spiritual
persons*, to answer the interrogatories of a lay tribunal,
General Boyer, to cut the matter short, banished them
from the country.

During our stay at the capital, a priest from the
country was brought up to answer a charge preferred
against him of keeping a note of ten dollars, offered by
the parents of a child to satisfy the baptismal fee.
Instead of returning nine dollars as change, he kept the
whole, on the principle that it ought to be given him!
The circumstance excited great indignation in the city,
and became a common subject of conversation. A brother
priest of the culprit's dined with us that day at the
public table, and when reproached with the transaction,
he coolly said, by way of defending his order, "There
is no rule without exceptions." There are undoubted
exceptions to the charge of *general* corruption. To say
nothing of the respectable Abbés of Cape Haytien and
Port-au-Prince, with whom we formed a friendship
when in those cities; we heard of a few other priests
who were much esteemed by their parishioners; and can
bear testimony to the zeal of one of them, residing at
Jacmel, in favour of general education, and the distribution of the holy scriptures; on which subjects he has
boldly stated his opinions in the principal journal of the
island. With regard to the ecclesiastical institutions of
the republic we may safely say, in conclusion, that if
the standing army be one cause of the degradation of
the people, the Church is surely another; and the sooner
it can be reformed, the better for religion, for morals,
and for the physical well being of the community.

In connexion with the state of the church, we must
not omit all mention of the protestants at Port-au-
Prince; a small band, but worthy of notice. There
are three congregations who possess dissenting chapels
within the limits of the city ; one of these are Baptists,
chiefly emigrants from America, who have service performed in the English language ; another is called
Methodist, but not in connexion with any recognized
body of Methodists, or under any control from abroad ;
and a third, Wesleyan Methodists, whose chapel is
the property of the Wesleyan Missionary Society of
London, and of whom James Hartwell, the representative of that society, is the esteemed and useful minister.
The entire number of professing protestants, French and
English, is about five hundred. The larger portion of
all these congregations are Anglo-Americans of the
middle class, or in the lowest walk of life; and many of
them, I am sorry to say, are far from adorning the
doctrines of the religion they profess, by a consistent
course of conduct. Instead of endeavouring to raise the
people around them from the moral degradation into
which a sort of semi-heathenism has plunged them,
they themselves give way to the prevailing corruptions,
and sink to the common level. There are some truly
pious people among the Wesleyans, who were awakened
to a sense of religion, under the preaching of the two
first missionaries of that denomination, about twenty-
five years since. The mission was suspended soon after
it commenced, owing to a grievous persecution from the
Romish priests ; but the fruits of its useful labours still
remain. We saw and conversed with several of these
primitive converts, and can bear testimony to their
simplicity, piety, and zeal : they form the nucleus of a

French church, which though very small at present as
to numbers, seems likely, under the new arrangements
of the mission, to increase. There is a station in the
mountains near Mirebalais, about thirty miles distant, in
connexion with them, at which about a hundred individuals occasionally meet to receive religious instruction.
The total number of professing protestants in all Hayti,
is presumed not to exceed twelve hundred.

In the year 1815, a visit of a religious character was
paid to this part of the island by Stephen Grellet, a
native of France, and minister of the Society of Friends,
who extended his travels to Cayes and Jacmel. The
former President, Alexander Pétion, received him with
great cordiality, and permitted him to preach to his
soldiers from the steps of the palace; himself and his
staff attending as auditors. The memory of this visit
still remains, and several persons bore testimony, in our
presence, to the preacher's faithfulness; many wishes
were also expressed that the Society of Friends might be
induced to send out some of its members to settle among
the people, and undertake to teach them. The door is
open to missionaries of all denominations, but whoever
enters on this field of labour must do it in faith, with
a single dependence on the Lord of the harvest for a
blessing. The fields at present are far from being
" white unto harvest;" and long and ardent toil and
watching, with much scoffing and neglect must be the
expected portion of every one who engages in the work.
Pious teachers of youth, men and women of enterprising
habits, who shall be able to converse and teach in the
French tongue, whom zeal in the cause of education
shall lead into the field; and whom no impediments can

daunt, or labour tire, are the individuals of whom Hayti stands in need, more especially at the present moment.

Intimately connected with the physical well-being of the Haytien population is the state and advancement of commerce among them. On this subject the papers furnished us by the government, throw considerable light. It cannot be expected, that a people lately engaged in a long and arduous struggle for independence, and but just released from the terrors of invasion, should have become at once commercial; but with all their disadvantages—with only a corrupt disbanded soldiery for cultivators of the soil; with an immense standing army; without education to raise them in the rank of civilised society, or even to stimulate them to industry, they maintain a respectable commercial standing among the nations.

The following table exhibits the quantity and sorts of produce exported from the island of Hayti in the years 1838 and 1839, distinguishing each year, with the value of the articles calculated in sterling money at the mean current rate of exchange for those years, of thirty-seven Haytien dollars to the Spanish doubloon, or about twelve Haytien dollars to the pound sterling. The weight of coffee, and other commodities, as given in pounds, represents a smaller amount than the actual weight according to our English scale, inasmuch as 100 lbs. Haytien are equal to 108 lbs. British. The coffee exported in 1838, instead of standing as it does in the table at 49,820,241 lbs. requires an addition of eight per cent. to make it European, and amounts to 53,805,857 lbs.

EXPORTATION FROM THE REPUBLIC OF HAYTI.

Produce.	1838.	1839.	Mean of the two years.	Market value exclusive of duty.	Value in sterling. money.
Coffee in lbs.....	49,820,241	37,889,092	43,854,666	Dol. 23 pr. 100 lbs.	£834,055
Cocoa ditto	453,418	477,414	465,416	.. 15½ ditto	6,019
Tobacco ditto ...	1,995,049	2,102,791	2,048,920	.. 30 ditto	51,222
Logwood ditto...	7,888,936	25,946,068	16,917,502	.. 26 per ton	18,325
Cotton ditto	1,170,175	1,635,420	1,402,792	.. 25 per 100 lbs.	29,223
Mahogany in ft.	4,880,873	5,908,477	5,392,175	.. 180 per 1000 ft.	81,955
Ginger in lbs. ..	39,076	36,366	37,721		
Horns in tale...	26,026	23,616	24,821		
Rags in lbs.	53,771	63,858	58,814		
Sirop de Batterie.	22,155	357,899	190,027	{	20,000
Hides in tale ...	21,978	31,866	26,982		
Cigars in 1000 ..	46	224	135		
Other products..	—	—	—.		
				Total	1,040,799

The crop of coffee varies greatly according to the season. In 1839, the season was favourable, and the return of coffee exported in 1840, was likely to exceed fifty millions of pounds weight. The year 1840 was a year of drought, and the quantity exported in 1841, was likely to be reduced to thirty millions. The average export of the country may be reckoned at fifty millions of pounds, rather less than more ; the present price free on board, at about 33s. per cwt. Coffee is the grand staple growth of the country, and comparing the present exportation of it, with that of the years previous to 1789, when the island was subject to the French, and the ground was cultivated by slave-labour, we shall have reason to believe that the quantity grown has experienced but a small diminution. The estimated amount of coffee exported during the latter years of slavery, was seventy millions of pounds. The consumption of that article in the island was then, probably but small ; it now enters into the wants of the common people; and allowing an additional consumption among them of a pound per week to each family of five persons, we raise the amount *produced* to fifty-eight millions of pounds, being a reduction of only twelve millions, or seventeen per cent. The next important article that claims attention is cotton. This was cultivated largely under slavery; the quantity formerly exported was more than 3,000,000 lbs., and as none is manufactured or brought into use in the island, the decrease is great. The trade in mahogany and dye-woods, has been of late years a vastly improving one, and bids fair to be a source of good profit to the merchant, and of revenue to the state. Some of the logs of mahogany shipped for England, have fetched enormous prices owing to their hardness and the exquisite fineness of their grain. A single tree of this description, sent over in two logs, was purchased, a few years since, by Broadwood and Co., pianoforte makers, for the extraordinary sum of £3000. The wood was cut into thin veneers, which received the finest polish and exhibited a surface of rare beauty. A log called the Prince Albert, lately shipped from Port-au-Prince, measured 800 feet, and realised the sum of 1950 Spanish dollars, or more than £400 sterling. The cost of mahogany on board at Port-au-Prince, including the export duty, of twenty-three Haytien dollars per thousand feet, is on an average of all sorts, about 220 Haytien dollars per thousand, or fourpence sterling per foot; a large cargo of a good quality meets an average nett sale price in England, of about sixteen-pence per foot.

Tobacco is an article of increased cultivation, and is claiming the earnest attention of proprietors and of the government. This commodity is chiefly grown in the north-east of the island, on lands peculiarly adapted to it, in the neighbourhood of Santiago. A considerable number of Anglo-Americans have settled in this region, and are engaged in its manufacture: leaf tobacco and cigars are at present the only preparations of it for foreign markets; but General Inginac has recently published a tract on the subject in which he strongly recommends a third preparation made ready for chewing, which he thinks may become an exportable commodity to a large extent. The price of tobacco has advanced in the Haytien market within the last ten years, from nine or ten dollars the quintal, to twenty-five or thirty dollars. A carreau, or square league of ground, cultivated in tobacco, will yield, on an average, three thousand pounds weight of the leaf: three labourers are sufficient to keep the field in order after the plants have been well cleaned; and in five months from the sowing of the seed, the harvest is ripe and ready for the purposes of commerce. Horns and hides of cattle were once exported in great quantities from the eastern part of the territory, and live cattle for slaughter in the neighbouring islands; but this trade has almost entirely ceased, owing to the narrow policy of England, France, and Spain; which nations have long forbidden a free intercourse between Hayti and their respective colonies. To the present moment no communication subsists between Hayti and Jamaica, though they lie within a day's sail of each other; and though a valuable exchange of commodities might often take place between them. England, a short time since, offered to open a trade between Hayti and the British West India islands; on the condition that certain preferences should be given to British merchants over those of other nations in the ports of Hayti: this the Haytien government very properly refused, and the negociation ended.

During our residence at Kingston, Jamaica, a sloop
under Haytien colours, entered the harbour in distress;
the vessel was permitted to come up to the quay for
repair, but no communication was allowed with the
shore : the captain and crew remained prisoners in their
own barque, and were not permitted to receive even a
friendly call from a stranger. The exclusiveness of other
nations begets exclusiveness in Hayti. No white man,
as we have seen, is permitted by the law of the republic
to hold a foot of land within its territory : no white
man can marry a Haytien woman, and thereby become
ontitlod to hor roal or personal estate ; and no white
man can trade without a special license, renewable
yearly, with a heavy fine ; nor indeed, generally speaking, can he trade at all without being associated with a
Haytien partner. Such restrictions as these tend to
exclude capital from the country, to paralyse industry,
and to prevent the increased cultivation of the soil.
But few Europeans can be found who are willing to
subject themselves to the fetters thus imposed upon
them. If a merchant of this class, which is sometimes
the case, marry a Haytien woman, and buy land, and
if he desire to preserve in his own hands the power of
disposing of his property during life or at death; he
takes a bond of his wife, or presumed wife, for the full
value of the land purchased, and then disposes of it at
his pleasure ; as the wife or children, who by law would
inherit the land, cannot take possession till the created
incumbrance has been paid off. By schemes like these,
the law is evaded as to some of its pernicious consequences; but it still maintains its supremacy in this
respect, that no white man can possess a freehold, in
his own right, in the soil.

The greater part of the land, in some of the extensive plains, is well adapted to the cultivation of sugar; and the exportation of that article was once very large. Previous to the year 1789, according to the table given by Bryan Edwards, in his history of the West Indies, the annual export of sugar from this colony, chiefly to the mother-country, was 1,296,360 cwts., or about 65,000 hogsheads of a ton each. This trade has entirely ceased; and on this circumstance is built the hypothesis, maintained in France, and in all the colonies where slavery, still exists, that freedom has ruined the island, and that slavery, and slavery alone can be relied on to ensure a sufficient supply of sugar for the markets of the old world. By far the larger part of the estates of the old proprietors went out of cultivation for want of hands, on the depopulation that followed the civil wars; but much land is still devoted to the sugar-cane, and yields an abundant supply of syrup, or uncrystalized sugar, and also of a spirit that is distilled from it, called tafia, which is consumed in the island to an astonishing extent. A great part of what once constituted the wealth of slave-proprietors, goes to supply the wants of the descendants of their slaves, who are now free and possess the soil. It is quite true, that these wants of the people pursue a wrong direction—that sugar is better than tafia—that it would be far better to export sugar, and purchase manufactured goods with the produce, than to consume the ardent spirit distilled from it: but this is a matter of taste with the consumers, whose comforts real or imaginary are bound up in the present system; and all we can say to them, as we might say to multitudes of the English, Scotch, and Irish, who pursue the same course, is, that in using strong drinks they greatly mistake the meaning of comfort and retard their own advancement in civil society. The syrup consumed is of excellent quality, as good and useful for all domestic purposes as sugar itself.

A review of the present exports of Hayti, brings us to a comparison of its foreign commerce with that carried on by other nations : nor shall we discover in it that ruinous deficiency of which the pro-slavery press of Europe and America, is so constantly complaining. The annual exports of the republic at the present day, exceed in value a million sterling. Its trade with the United States of America, was greater a few years since than it is at the present time. In the year 1839, the United States imported from Hayti to the value of 2,347,556 dollars ; and exported thence to the value of 1,815,212 dollars, whilst from *all the British West Indies* in the same period, the imports were only 1,835,227 dollars, the exports 1,522,347 dollars, leaving a balance of imports in favour of Hayti, as compared with that of our colonies, of more than 500,000 dollars! In the same year, Hayti sent more merchandize to the United States than almost any European power, except Great Britain, France, and Russia, and nearly as much as the latter. During the year 1840, the imports of foreign goods into the United States, amounted to 107,141,519 dollars. The exports to 132,085,946 dollars, or £27,000,000 sterling. The population of the United States is twenty times as large as that of Hayti: its trade is only twenty-seven times as large.

In the year 1840, *the declared value* of British and Irish produce and manufactures exported from this country to Hayti, was £251,979, a larger amount than it sent either to Denmark, to Prussia, or to our own

trading ports of Malta; and more than half as much as
it exported either to Mexico or to the great empire of
China! The total value of the *produce and manufactures* of the United Kingdom, exported from this
country in 1839, was £50,060,970. The total mean
value of produce exported from Hayti, in the years
1838 and 1839, as we have seen in the previous table,
was £1,040,799. The population of Hayti may be
estimated at 850,000; that of Great Britain and Ireland
is twenty-seven millions.

Thus we see that the exports of the United Kingdom,
considered relatively in proportion to the number of
its inhabitants, are as one-eighty-five to one; those
from the United States of America, as one-sixty-five
to one; those from Hayti, as one-twenty-five to one.
So that Hayti, poor, and despised as she is, has a
commerce, *in native produce*, nearly three-fourths
as large, *in proportion to her population*, as our own
United Kingdom, which is the great manufacturing mart
of the world; and seven-eighths as large as that of the
United States, where the staple exports are produced
by the labour of three millions of slaves! The only
disadvantage to Hayti in this comparison is, that Great
Britain has an immense carrying trade: Hayti has
none: but how can she be expected to raise a commerce
of this kind without capital; and how can capital be
created whilst she continues to exclude foreigners from
her soil, and whilst her institutions tend rather to depress
than to encourage the industry of her people?

The following table exhibits a view of part of the
commerce of Hayti for the year 1840. It gives the
imports and exports of its two principal shipping ports
only. When it was ut into my hands, the returns

had not been received from the other ports of the island :—

1840.—GROSS RETURN OF BRITISH AND FOREIGN TRADE.

PORT-AU-PRINCE.

	ARRIVED.				DEPARTED.			
Nation.	No. of Vessels.	Tons.	Crew.	Invoice value of Cargoes.	No. of Vessels.	Tons.	Crew.	Invoice value of Cargoes.
British......	31	5218	290	£190,627	31	4925	247	£159,750
French......	15	3033	176	69,870	23	4883	260	131,054
German	18	2813	172	101,400	20	3080	184	94,980
Belgian	1	300	15		1	300	15	7,300
United States	75	9167	573	109,122	75	9143	538	98,830
Swedish	2	281	17	2,500	2	281	17	1570
	142	20,812	1243	£473,519	152	22,612	1261	£493,484

CAPE HAYTIEN.

Nation.	No. of Vessels.	Tons.	Crew.	Invoice value of Cargoes.	No. of Vessels.	Tons.	Crew.	Invoice Value of Cargoes.
British.......	12	1671	95	£43,183	14	2045	113	£46,642
Haytien ...	3	275	18	790	3	275	18	1656
French......	15	2402	145	56,097	14	2179	132	59,945
German.....	7	1290	81	44,118	6	1170	72	49,499
American...	31	4015	176	46,030	31	4070	181	53,857
Danish	2	126	16	3075	2	126	16	1030
	70	9779	531	£193,293	70	9865	532	£212,629

Port-au-Prince and Cape Haytien . Imports £666,812.
. . . . Exports £706,063.

1840.—Exchange first six months, ten dollars to the pound sterling.

Second six months, twelve and a half dollars.

1841.—Thirteen dollars to thirteen and a half.

The trade of Port-au-Prince, the capital, on an average of years, is nearly half that of the whole island : doubling therefore the amount of British goods imported, we have £380,000 *as the invoice value* of cargoes sent from the United Kingdom : take it at less than that sum—say £320,000, and it corresponds substantially with the *declared value* of the same goods at our own Custom-house, only adding 25 per cent. for profit, charges, and risk.

It is greatly to be lamented, that the commerce of Hayti, large as it is by comparison with that of many other nations, should remain so limited and stationary as it has done. Were the industry of the people brought properly to bear upon the soil, and were the juice of the sugar-cane manufactured into sugar for exportation, instead of being converted into a deleterious spirit which injures and degrades the consumers, the exchangeable products of the country might in a few years be multiplied five-fold—its debt to France, now a heavy burden, might be speedily paid off—its depreciated currency might be raised to par; and its wealth and resources might be greatly increased.

The great and leading grievance complained of in the republic, is its enormous debt to France. The subsidy guaranteed by treaty to France in 1825, as an indemnification to the former French colonists, for their estates, was extorted at the cannon's mouth. The amount promised for this object was one-hundred and fifty millions of francs; and for the public edifices and fortifications, *(by a secret treaty)* thirty millions of francs more! Of this enormous subsidy, sixty millions of francs were actually paid in coffee and hard cash before the close of the year 1828, leaving a nominal debt then due to France, of one hundred and twenty millions of francs, or £5,000,000 sterling. The treasury of the island was by this time become exhausted, and the people discontented; no new taxes could be imposed; and it was found necessary, at the risk to the state of being pronounced bankrupt, to discontinue all further payments.

In the year 1838, Louis Phillippe finding it
impossible to secure the execution of the treaty of
1825, entered into fresh negociations with President
Boyer; and by a second treaty, reduced the debt
claimable by the French government to half its former
amount, or sixty millions of francs. In the years
1838, 1839, and 1840, the Haytien government paid
off by yearly instalments, 4,500,000 francs, leaving
an actual balance, due at the commencement of 1841,
of 55,500,000 francs, or £2,312,500. Besides this
debt, on account of the original subsidy, the payment
of which is to be by instalments, and to terminate in
1867 ; the Haytien government owes a considerable
sum to the monied interests of France, on account of
a loan of thirty millions of francs, advanced by Lafitte
and Co., in the year 1825, which amounted at the same
period to fourteen millions of francs, or £583,334 ;
and which is now bearing interest at the rate of three
per cent. per annum. This debt is in 14,000 coupons
of a thousand francs each, of which number the government pays off at least six hundred every year. It does
so by buying them up at their present reduced value
of 600 francs per coupon, instead of 1000 francs, which
is the nominal value. The loan was contracted for on
the condition that the borrowers should pay a thousand
francs for every eight hundred francs received in cash
down. When the house of Lafitte and Co. became
embarrassed, the head partner solicited President Boyer,
to purchase of him a thousand coupons which he held in
his own right, at *the cost price* of 800 francs each; the
President, instead of doing so, generously bought them at
the price guaranteed by the government, allowing him
to make a personal profit of £8000 by the transaction.

Such a circumstance reflects honour on the Haytien government, and tends to confirm the public judgment in its favour, as it manifests a determination on its part to pay every shilling of its present enormous debt. The total of that debt, with, and without interest, at the commencement of 1841, was £2,895,834!

The government paper money in circulation, at the same period, was 3,500,000 Haytien dollars; and there remained in the public treasury of Spanish dollars, 1,300,000, which at the present depreciated value of the paper money, would be about sufficient to buy it up. The metallic currency of the island, is about 2,000,000 Haytien dollars, equal in bullion to 500,000 Spanish dollars. All the *import duties* of the island are levied in gold and silver, and serve to pay off the debt to France, which consents to receive its annual instalments only in specie. These duties, amounted in 1837, at which period the treasury was empty, to :—

701,166 dollars.

in	1838	to	768,419	
„	1839	„	843,883	
„	1840	„	900,000	{ Account not yet made up, but not less than this sum.

3,213,468

Deduct paid to France in these four years } 2,000,000

1,213,468. leaving in the treasury when the account shall be made up, a sum certainly equal to the above, amounting in sterling value, to £250,000.

Let us now look at the income and expenditure of the country in Haytien dollars, leaving out of consideration

the import duties received in Spanish money, which are
raised to satisfy the instalments due to France.

REVENUE.		EXPENDITURE.	
	Haytien Dollars.		Haytien Dollars.
1837 .	1,380,356	1837 . .	2,176,792
1838 . .	1,918,458	1838 .	2,273,768
1839 .	1,840,988	1839 . .	2,112,290
1840, (estimated,)	1,900,000	1840, (estimated,)	2,000,000
	7,039,802		8,562,850
		Deduct revenue	7,039,802
			1,523,048

Thus we see that in four years there was a deficiency arising from the excess of expenditure above the
income, of 1,523,048 Haytien dollars ; and a surplus, in
specie, from the import duties, above the sum called
for to satisfy the claims of France, of 1,213,468
Spanish dollars. The surplus in *actual value* is much
larger than the deficiency. Hayti, therefore, independent of her home debt in depreciated paper, is solvent:
her government, even on the present scale of income and
expenditure, can go on, gradually extinguishing its
foreign debt, and increasing its stores of gold and silver.
But she owes a large debt to her people. The deficiency arising in former years from the excess of expenditure above income has been met by an issue of paper
money, and this money has gone on increasing, till it
amounts in nominal value to 3,500,000 dollars. The
paper is issued as representing Spanish dollars ; but it
has gone gradually depreciating, till it has become worth
only one-third of its specified value. A doubloon
worth sixteen Spanish dollars, will often readily purchase
in the market forty-eight dollars in paper. What

under these circumstances, ought the Haytien government to do? Should it buy up its own paper money
at this immense discount, and replace it, with a currency
of gold and silver on a par with that of Europe and
America? By such a measure it would compound
like a bankrupt, and break faith with its subjects:
or should it strive by measures of reduction and
economy to put itself in the situation of being able to
withdraw a portion of it every year from circulation,
and thus restore the remainder to par? The latter is
the only plan that an honest government can pursue.
Numerous suggestions on the compounding plan, have
been made to the President who has wisely rejected
them all. Let us now see how the opposite course
would act. The income of Hayti, *independent of its
import duties,* has gone on gradually increasing since
1837, whilst its expenditure has gradually lessened.
By a very small measure of further retrenchment and
economy the two sides of the balance sheet may be
made equal. The government notes now in circulation
amount to 3,500,000 dollars; the cash in the treasury
to 1,400,000 dollars. The absolute deficiency, therefore, valuing the notes at par, is little more than two
millions of dollars. Supposing it impossible to reduce
the expenditure, so far as to obtain a surplus of income
from the common sources of internal revenue; and no
one who looks at the immense standing army can allow
this for a moment; there are still within the reach of
the executive ample means of liquidating this debt,
without infringing in any degree on the national honour.
The annual excess of income in Spanish money paid
at the custom house for import duties, after satisfying
the claims of France, is 300,000 dollars. Why suffer

this surplus to be added every year to the cash of the
treasury, where it lies in mortmain? How far better,
instead of insisting for the future on the payment of
the import duties altogether in gold, to allow the
merchant to pay them part in gold, and part in notes—
say 700,000 dollars in cash, and 200,000 in paper! By
this means, one-tenth of the paper debt of the country
would be extinguished every year, as at the end of ten
years all the notes in circulation will have been withdrawn, except 1,500,000 dollars, and the government,
like a good banker, will have cash in its coffers to pay
these on demand. In ten years Hayti would be out of
debt. For every one of the ten years that such a
transaction would be in progress, the state would have
100,000 dollars in gold and silver to bestow on works
of public utility : this sum would more than equal in
value the 200,000 dollars of paper money withdrawn ;
and though the circulating medium would be less in
nominal amount, it would represent and give value to a
larger amount of commercial transactions than before.
In connexion with this change, the present debased
silver coin of the country must be converted into coin
of the same value as other countries : this would be no
loss to the holders, because if made of three or four times
as much value as before, it would purchase three or four
times as much merchandise. To effect these improvements with advantage to all parties, and to regulate
the exchange with foreign nations, there should be
established a national bank. The House of Assembly
is crying out against the hardship of paying all the
import duties in cash, and begs the President to initiate
a law to relieve the country from this pressure ; the
President wishes for a national bank, and entreats the

other branches of the legislature to assist him in forming such an establishment on a solid basis. The above plan would meet every difficulty; and, if carried out with judgment, might probably be made to satisfy all parties. By such a measure, the credit of the republic would be sustained. The merchant would be benefited by being put into possession of greater value for his paper money than he imagines it to be worth; as this paper, in proportion as it lessened in amount, would go on increasing in value, till it arrived at par; the consumer would be benefited, because the merchant, from his increased capital and security, would be satisfied with less profit, and goods would thus fall in price; and all classes of the public functionaries would be benefited, because they would receive better pay from the increased value of the currency, in which their respective salaries would be paid.

To complete our view of the finances of the republic of Hayti, it only remains to us to exhibit *the details* of its income and expenditure. The following table gives a general result of the receipts and disbursements of the treasury for the year 1839:—

RECEIPTS.

At the Ports of	Import duties in Gold.		Export and Territorial duties.		All other taxes.		Total Revenue.	
	doll.	c.	doll.	c.	doll.	c	doll.	c.
Port-au-Prince...	450,130	92	516,126	41	290,396	98	1,256,654	31
Jeremie........	5,219	42	13,679	4	16,845	1	35,743	47
Cayes	108,747	76	175,628	85	60,205	15	344,581	76
Jacmel	64,824	67	133,334	12	28,927	96	227,086	75
Gonaives	26,622	59	77,267	5	35,127	66	139,017	30
Cape-Haytien ..	156,947	1	201,957	71	92,466	3	451,370	75
Porte-Platte....	18,422	66	33,037	96	37,707	4	89,167	66
Santo Domingo.	47,107	5	57,998	5	36,144	47	141,249	57
	878,022	8	1,209,029	19	597,820	30	2,684,871	57

Duties on Imports...... 843,883
Duties on Consignments 34,139

DISBURSEMENTS.

Public works.	Civil service.	Army and Navy.	National Debt	Total.
doll. c.	doll. c.	doll. c.	doll. c.	doll. c.
39,889 60	610,699 38	1,378,611 34	469,373 63	2,498,573 95
Paper money burnt...............................				133,381
				2,631,954 95

BALANCE SHEET.

	dollars c.
There remained in the public treasury, 31st Dec. 1838	766,246 12
General receipts of the Republic, during the year 1839	2,684,871 58
Notes issued during the same year .	333,800 0
Total .	3,784,917 70

	dollars c.	
Disbursements of the year 1839	2,498,573 95	
Notes of issue burnt during the year	133,381 0	
		2,631,954 95
Remaining in the treasury, 31st Dec. 1839.		1,152,962 75

DETAIL OF THE MONEY REMAINING IN THE TREASURY.

	Foreign money	National money.
At Port-au-Prince .	801,770 87	139,498 91
„ Jeremie . . .	1721 83	7,261 45
„ Cayes . . .	4249 92	60,628 10
„ Jacmel . .	9841 98	54,640 68
„ Gonaives . . .	1181 73	5247 16
„ Cape Haytien . .	18,715 91	8933 67
„ Porte Platte . .	5186 92	4636 48
„ Santo Domingo .	7447 56	9217 5
" Envois de fonds par mandate a regler entre la caisse du Port-au-Prince et celles du Cap Haytien et des Cayes" . . .		12,782 52
Monies of all sorts .	Dol. 1,152,962 75	

The balance sheet of the republic, for the year 1840,
would exhibit a statement more favourable than the one

just given; but I could not obtain a copy of it before
we left the country.

Our next statistical inquiry, one of great importance,
relates to the employments of the people. A report is
sent every year to the President, from the commanders
of the several *arrondissements*, or districts; in which
they profess to show how the lands are cultivated—what
progress has been made in agriculture and commerce—
how many estates are worked—how many abandoned—
and how many freeholders occupy land in their own
right. This branch of statistical and general information, if carried out by enlightened men, would prove
highly valuable in any country, as illustrating its
condition; but, unfortunately for Hayti, the men to
whom this task is confided are many of them illiterate,
with narrow views, who enter upon it unwillingly, and
whose statements are consequently often meagre, ill-
arranged, and most unsatisfactory. The reports from all
the arrondissements for several years past, were put into
my hands by the government, and I have endeavoured
to compile from them a general statement; which, if it
does not satisfy the reader, and put him in possession of
all the facts which such reports ought to convey, will at
least throw some light on the present state and condition
of the Haytien people, and tend to silence the unjust and
ill-founded clamour of pro-slavery partizans against them.
It should first be premised, that the disbanded soldiers of
the armies that served in the revolutionary and civil wars,
were rewarded, at the commencement of the republic
under President Boyer, with a grant of nine acres
of land each; the non-commissioned and superior officers
receiving more in proportion to their rank. The labourers
on Christophe's estates in the north of the island, availed

themselves of this donative, and settled on their own freeholds, thus imitating the conduct of their brethren of the south, who had already done so in great numbers. Many of the large coffee estates, and some of the sugar plantations of the old colonists, were broken up and parted piece-meal to the new claimants; and land was given on mountain passes, where no cultivation had ever before been carried on. From this cause the small properties, now in existence, are very numerous. In the year 1839, there were altogether 46,610 such properties under *good* cultivation. The number may not be exact, as no returns on this head were made from the arrondissements of Tiburon, St. Jague, and St. Mark, and the total result is only arrived at by approximation.

On the subject of population we shall have to speak presently; but taking its amount for argument's sake to be 800,000, and the number of inhabitants employed in agriculture to be 700,000, or seven-eighths of the whole; which, to persons who have visited the island, will not appear an improper estimate; we find fifteen individuals to each rural property. A large number of small estates are left out of this account, which are said to be *badly* cultivated, or neglected. Taking the number of each separate family on an average, at five persons, husband, wife, and three children, we arrive at the conclusion, that the head of every third family in the state is engaged in cultivating his own freehold; a proportion of independent proprietors, such as perhaps scarcely any other country in the world can exhibit. The number of acres cultivated by these small proprietors, varies from nine to thirty; many of them keep horses, asses, cows, and goats: they raise sufficient provisions of the bread kind, such as yams, plantains, and bananas, for the main

support of their families; they kill hogs for meat, and
they dispose of their coffee, cotton, hemp, castor oil, and
fruit, at the public market for money, to purchase
clothing, furniture, and other necessaries. The houses
they live in, though poorly furnished, are decent habitations; and many of them have gardens attached,
neatly fenced in with bamboo, or with logwood, or aloe
hedges. The labourers of the country, who with their
families constitute the other two-thirds of the rural
population, are of two classes, those who work for a
given rate of wages, and those who work for shares of
the produce on the estates of the large proprietors. The
latter are probably the most numerous, and deserve a
particular mention. The Rural Code recognizes and
defines the rights and duties of master and servant, and
interferes with the latter in a manner so severe and
arbitrary, as to have lost its effect. The common people
refuse to sell their labour subject to its provisions, or
utterly disregard them. The labourers who work on
shares, to receive part of the produce at the end of the
season, are mostly located on the properties where they
work, and occupy the huts and cabins, which, under the
old *regime* were inhabited by the slaves.

Some gangs of labourers work for one-half of the
total produce of the estate, raising food for themselves
at their own expense; and others for a quarter of the
produce, under an agreement that the proprietor should
keep them in provisions. Which plan is the most
economical to the labourer and his family, is doubtful:
on some estates, one plan is probably the best, and on
other estates the other; but that both are prejudicial
to the landed proprietors and to the country at large, is
very evident. Nothing but the resemblance which such

a system bears to freedom and independence could recon-
cile the people to its continuance for any great length of
time : the truth is, that notwithstanding the self-conse-
quence it imparts to the labourer, making him, in his
own estimation, almost as great and important as a
freeholder in his own right; it works badly for all the
parties concerned. The master cannot say to his men,
go into such a field and dig cane holes, the clouds are
gathering and we must get in the young plants—or
weed such a field,—or prune the coffee trees; neither
can he send a band of young people at his pleasure to
pick the coffee berries as they ripen, or select the bad
berries, when pulped and dried, from the good ones.
Every servant, if we may so speak, is master of his own
house and his own hours; and considers himself at
liberty to work with his family almost at what time,
and in what manner he pleases. He will not always
submit to the dictum of the proprietor, nor always
conform to the regulations imposed on him for the
general good.

The labourers, from this cause, become jealous of each
other : if they work together they cannot agree among
themselves, as to the exact quantity of labour to be performed by each : one man is weaker than another; one
is more disposed to drink and saunter, and be idle, than
another. The whole twenty families, in common, are to
share half the gross produce, or one-fourth of it, as the
case may be; but who shall measure the exact proportion
that falls in justice to the lot of each ?

To remedy the inconvenience arising from this want
of agreement among the labourers, as to the exact part
which every one should perform; the proprietor often
finds it necessary to divide his fields among them, allow-

ing one family five acres, by task work, another ten, and a third twenty, according to the nature of the land, and the sort of produce to be raised upon it. By this means, he loses all the benefits of the concentration of labour to particular spots at particular seasons, and much loss of crop ensues ; or if he wants, and is resolved to have some needful work done in haste, which requires a larger number of labourers than are allotted to it, he has to bribe others to come in and help them, by the offer of a drink of rum or tafia. The aim of a proprietor is to get as many families to band together as can act in concert without jarring, or jealousy, and to induce them, by kindness, to do as much work as possible for his own interest as well as theirs : in some cases, he succeeds tolerably well ; but one man disposed to be sullen or idle, or who is unable to work from sickness, throws the whole system into disorder. One great evil of it is this, that every labourer knows that he does not suffer alone for his own idleness or neglect: his fellow-labourers share the consequences of his misconduct in some degree, and his master in a still greater. If he alone had to bear the loss, he would be more disposed to fill up his time diligently, and do his best.

The Rural Code professes to meet all cases of misconduct arising out of this state of things, and gives summary power to justices of the peace to inflict mulcts and penalties. To say nothing however, of the loss of time, and of the vexation to both parties, in constantly repairing to a justice for his decision, the proprietor himself is afraid to act on this principle to any extent, lest by doing so, he should lose his labourers altogether. How different is the system of wages, and how much more advantageous to the labourers themselves ! One governing mind surveys a large property; and, taking advantage of circumstances and seasons, directs the labourers, few or many, as the occasion may require, to the very spot and to the very kind of work where their labour may find the most profitable direction: every labourer devotes his skill to that particular employment in which he most excels, and receives pay in proportion to the work done, and to the manner of doing it. By this means a larger produce is raised, and a larger share of that produce goes to the hands that assist in raising it.

A correspondence has been carried on in one of the public journals, between some of the proprietors of sugar estates in the *Cul de Sac* as to which is most beneficial, the system of shares, or the system of wages. Political economy I think would answer the question, without any hesitation, in favour of wages. To this point, the minds of proprietors are fast tending; and to this point, the labourers themselves, afraid as they are of losing a jot of their independence, are in some places reluctantly coming round. The military system encourages idleness in one direction; that of working by shares on the produce of estates seems to bestow a bounty upon it in another; ignorance deepens the evil by teaching men to be content with a low state of physical existence; and the common people, from the operation of all these various causes of discouragement and decay, exhibit an aspect far from attractive.

The poet Goldsmith, in describing the peasantry of Switzerland, has too correctly, and with much greater truth, described the condition of the people of Hayti.

" Unknown to them, when sensual pleasures cloy
　To fill the languid pause with finer joy ;
　Unknown those powers that raise the soul to flame,
　Catch every nerve, and vibrate through the frame.
　Their level life is but a smouldering fire,
　Unquench'd by want, unfann'd by strong desire ;
　Unfit for raptures ; or if raptures cheer
　On some high festival of once a year,
　In wild excess the vulgar breast takes fire,
　Till, buried in debauch, the bliss expire.
　But not their joys alone thus coarsely flow ;
　Their morals, like their pleasures, are but low ;
　For, as refinement stops, from sire to son,
　Unaltered, unimproved, the manners run ;
　And love and friendships finely pointed dart
　Falls blunted from each indurated heart."

THE TRAVELLER.

A people circumstanced like the Haytiens, having
such ready means of obtaining a livelihood might be
thought likely to increase and multiply beyond the
common ratio of countries, where the soil is less fertile,
and the seasons are less congenial. But idleness, and
vice are a curse 'on any land; whilst honest industry
and enterprise often succeed in converting a barren soil
into fruitful fields.

The population of Hayti increases, but it does not,
it cannot, increase so fast as it would do, if the citizens
were a moral race, and if the institutions of the state,
instead of depressing industry, could be said to encourage
it. The amount of population is a problem which no
writer has been able correctly to solve : the number of
inhabitants in what was once the Spanish part of the
island is pretty well ascertained by continuing the mode
of taking a census at certain periods which has long
prevailed there : in the French territory, where the
population is most dense, the number can only be
arrived at by approximation. A census was ordered

by the government to be taken many years ago in the French province; but the ordinance was issued at a most unhappy time. The treaty had just then been completed with France, to grant to that country an immense subsidy as a compensation to the ex-colonists for the loss of their territory; and the people being afraid that a census was only intended as a preliminary to a poll-tax to assist in paying it, threw every obstacle in its way, and the plan was abandoned. No systematic attempt of the kind has since been made.

In the year 1789, before the revolutionary war had begun its horrible ravages, the people of the French provinces were thus enumerated:—whites, 30,831; free people of colour, 24,000; town slaves, 46,000; rural slaves, 434,429; total, 535,260.

The losses of the Haytiens from the year 1791 to 1804, when Dessalines proclaimed the independence of the island, and made himself Emperor, were incalculably great: by battles, massacres, blood-hounds, drowning, and other atrocities, the population had been thinned to a dreadful extent. By a census, such as it was, taken during the short reign of this tyrant the whole population, black and coloured, (the whites had disappeared), was estimated at about 380,000, shewing a disappearance in thirteen years of more than 150,000 people!

During the destructive civil war that succeeded the death of Dessalines which was carried on between the north and the south, under Christophe and Pétion, a great number of the people fell in battle, and the springs of industry were everywhere relaxed: the popu-lation, however, rather increased than diminished; an estimate formed, by Christophe, about the middle of his reign, represented the total amount at 393,000. Since

that period, thirty years have elapsed; the country has
been mostly at peace; the disbanded soldiery have
become freeholders, or returned to labour in the fields of
the new proprietors—and the population has greatly
augmented; according to the ordinary rate of increase
under favourable circumstances, it ought at the present
moment, to amount on the French side to eight hundred thousand; and, including the Spanish provinces,
to at least a million. Humboldt estimates the present
population of the whole island at eight hundred thousand,
and this estimate, from all the inquiries I have made,
and the information afforded me, seems more likely than
any other to be correct. The population of the Spanish,
or eastern side, is not larger, or very little so, than when
the country was a colony of France: this arises from
the large migration of later years from that part of the
island to the French provinces, in consequence of the
trade in cattle having ceased to afford them employment. Among the papers that I solicited of the government, were returns of the registered births, burials,
and marriages in the whole island for the last ten
years: these were promised me, but not being ready
when we left the island, the Secretary of State, General
Inginac, promised to send them after me to England:
they have not yet, however, arrived; and if in my possession, it is very doubtful whether they would throw
any extraordinary light on the question, owing to the
acknowledged vast deficiency in the registration of
deaths. One document of this kind, and only one, has
been put into my hands: this relates to the Spanish provinces, and is tolerably clear and explicit. I here insert
it, together with the comments of the able senator who
took the pains to compile it.

DEPARTMENT OF THE SOUTH-EAST.

Statistical Table of the Nine Communes of this Department.

ANNO 1838.

Communes.	Births.	Deaths.	Marriages.	Estimated population.
Santa Domingo	506	218	61	14,674
Monte Plata	65	28	15	1885
Bayaguana	33	8	9	957
San Cristabal	220	82	25	6380
Higuey	80	33	4	2320
Seybo	279	133	35	8091
Samana	52	38	10	1508
Llanos	79	33	10	2291
Bony	138	41	20	4002
	1452	614	189	42,108

DEPARTMENT OF THE NORTH-EAST.

Statistical Table of the Nine Communes of this Department.

ANNO 1838.

Communes.	Births.	Deaths.	Marriages.	Estimated population.
Santiago	647	241	128	18,567
La Vega	287	132	54	8323
Moca	298	102	66	8642
Cotuy	106	49	11	3074
Monte Christi	49	7	8	1421
Porte Platte	233	89	30	6757
San José de las Matas	147	8	33	4263
Macory	180	85	32	5220
Altamira	59	3	17	1711
	2006	716	379	57,978

REMARKS BY THE COMPILER.

" The population of the above department, after adding the increase arising from births, amounts to 57,978; but as there are some evident omission on the part of the officers who keep the registers, we may safely reckon it at sixty thousand. The larger proportionate increase in the north above the south, arises from the fact, that the people continue to emigrate from the southern communes to the north of the island, where the cultivation of coffee and tobacco goes on fast increasing. I say fast increasing, but I here only speak comparatively, as taking into consideration the favourableness of the climate, and the fertility of the ground, *the produce ought to be four-fold what it is.*

" The children born in wedlock, as compared with those that are illegitimate, are as one in four.

" There remains in the department of the north-east but one single primary school.

" Crime being everywhere," continues the compiler, " in the inverse of civilisation, what are the best means of improving the condition of the commonwealth ? The President is an enlightened man, but the payment of the national debt absorbs the attention of his government. He who has succeeded in putting an end to our civil dissensions, who has united, under the banner of liberty, the whole territory of the republic, who has happily negotiated the country's independence, cannot fail, as soon as circumstances permit, to turn his thoughts to those points that concern the civil advancement of the people. He will fix his attention—

" 1st. Upon a good system of popular education.

" 2nd. Upon a penitentiary system for the reform of criminals.

" 3rd. On a better police and gen'd'armerie.

" 4th. On the establishment of municipal corporations, for self-government in the towns.

" 5th. On the augmentation of the national income, and the diminution of its expenditure, which will prove to be no paradox, but a reality to be readily accomplished for the public good—by which means the government will be better administered, the public treasures will be increased ; and those who rule, and those that are ruled, will both be increasingly happy.

" 6th. On a plan for the encouragement of good domestic servants, and the punishment of bad ones.

" 7th. On the priesthood—good and indefatigable pastors, who shall preach sound morality and the doctrines of the gospel; and who, without distinction, shall be paid for their services out of the public treasury.

" 8th. On giving protection to the solemn institution of marriage, to institutions of benevolence, to agriculture, commerce, and industry.

" 9th. On improved public roads and highways."

The foregoing observations of one of the most enlightened men of Hayti, who now fills the honourable office of President of the Senate, and who knows, better than most men, the real state and condition of his fellow-countrymen, are entitled to the serious consideration of his own government, and of all persons who have the welfare of Hayti at heart.   In glancing at the tables above given, it cannot fail to strike even the superficial reader, how evidently untrustworthy are the registers of deaths.   If the increase of population be every year estimated by the increase of births over deaths, as exhibited in the civil records, its progress must appear enormous; but this is not the case in the Spanish territory, as a census, according to long custom, is taken every year, and serves to check and correct the registers.   It then appears, that the eastern provinces, which, in point of territory, embrace two-thirds of the island, has a scattered population of only 102,000 persons.   Well may the extensive plain, which the eye of Columbus surveyed with so much astonishment from the top of the mountains in the range of Monte Christi, be denominated "La despob-

lada," or the uninhabited! Were the French provinces
of Hayti no better peopled, in proportion, than those
on the Spanish side, the whole island would be one comparative wilderness. We have no means of arriving
satisfactorily at what is the actual total number of the
inhabitants on the French side: but the most probable
conjecture would lead us to consider it about three-
quarters of a million, and thus to fix the entire population of Hayti at 850,000. The government of the
country represents it at a million.

The registered births, which are the record of
baptisms, and therefore presumed to be correct, are,
according to the above tables, as one to thirty of the
presumed population; a calculation which agrees very
nearly with the experience of Great Britain and some
other nations. Allowing the population of Hayti, as a
new country, to increase in a somewhat greater proportion than that of Great Britain, which we can
scarcely doubt to be the case; we no longer wonder that
it should have nearly doubled itself in thirty years. The
marriages are very few indeed, amounting only to one in
two hundred and twenty-three annually. In England
and Wales, in 1831, the proportion was as one to one
hundred and twenty-three; and it must be observed,
that in the Spanish provinces, from which the above
enumeration is given, marriages are supposed to be
much more common than in other parts. What a
mournful exhibition is thus presented to us of the morals
of Hayti! How earnestly must the friends of freedom,
and of good order in civil society, desire amelioration in
the institutions of the country!

CHAPTER VII.

DURING our stay at Port-au-Prince we sometimes rode
out on horseback among the neighbouring villas, or to
take a glance at the sugar plantations at some distance
from the city. On three or four occasions, we were
invited to partake of country hospitalities ; and we
greatly enjoyed both the company we met with, and
the picturesque scenery we surveyed. Doctor Smith, a
physician, son-in-law to General Inginac, has a handsome villa about two miles from the capital, where we
passed a long and pleasant day. Early in the morning,
a travelling carriage drawn by two mules and a strong
jackass all abreast, and guided by a postilion, conveyed
us to his house. The custom of the country prescribes
a cup of coffee at rising from bed : *a second breakfast,*
served *a la fourchette,* with cutlets, boiled rice, sweet
potatoes, hot bread, tea and coffee, follows at eleven
o'clock : the dinner hour is often protracted to six or
seven o'clock in the evening. On this occasion, we met
at the dinner table several gentlemen, one of whom was
the President of the Senate before-mentioned, and
another the *procureur* or State-attorney of Jacmel, who

seemed gratified in being able to answer our inquiries
with regard to the habits and condition of the people
in his own district. The President of the Senate, when
a young man, accompanied Stephen Grellet, a minister
of the Society of Friends, alluded to in a former chapter
of this work, to a religious meeting which he held in
the Freemasons Hall; and remarked, in reference to
the circumstance, which seemed to have made a deep
impression on his memory, " I assure you that your
Society is held in much veneration here." All the party
present treated us with the utmost kindness; and expressed their gratification at receiving visitors who
desired the welfare of their native land, and who came
to examine their institutions with a friendly eye. In
walking over the doctor's grounds, we saw a favourite
riding horse lying on the ground, with his thigh and
leg frightfully swollen, from the bite of a tarantula.
In the evening we made a short excursion to a neighbouring property, laid out in beautiful order, and com-
bining many advantages of nature and art. The
gardens were admirably kept up; the trees that
adorned them were lofty and noble; the tropical shrubs
were in full flower, and the grand ocean formed part
of the prospect. The weather was pleasantly cool, the
thermometer varying from 71o at sunrise, to 80o at noon.

On our return at night to the city, we witnessed one
of those strange sights which are common in Roman
Catholic countries, but which we had never seen before.
The carnival of " Shrove Tuesday," called here the Mar-
digras, had commenced, and the streets for this and
several succeeding days were abandoned to public
amusement. Great numbers of the people were
dressed in masquerade, some in rich and expensive

oriental costume, and moved about on foot, on horseback, and in carriages, either alone, or in groups, and
silently saluted the passers by, or entered into houses
to receive such entertainment as the inmates proffered.
A few groups were attended by musicians with the
flute and violin, and bands of music paraded the city.
Some of the dresses were exceedingly grotesque, and'
gave rise to repeated sallies of mirth ; but there was
more of order and decency in the whole proceedings
than could have been reasonably looked for in such a
community.   There is much more foolery, according to
the testimony of travellers, in Naples and the Italian
cities, than we observed in Port-au-Prince.

One of the pleasantest journeys we performed was to
the extensive sugar plain, called *Le Cul de Sac.* Early
one morning, accompanied by our friend the Wesleyan
missionary, and a servant as our guide, we set off on
horseback to Mocquet, a property belonging to three
brothers, who cultivate this and another estate in sugar,
and manufacture the syrup into tafia, a sort of fiery rum,
much in favour with the common people as a customary
beverage.   This estate has a hundred and twenty acres
in cane, and with the syrup expressed from it, and with
what is bought in addition from the small proprietors
around them, the owners make 1200 barrels of spirit
yearly.   After breakfast, accompanied by our host,
who ordered his private carriage and horses to be made
ready for our use, we travelled over a good road, formed
in the bottom of a watercourse, which was now dry,
to an estate belonging to the Treasurer-general of
the island.   Here we found the sugar mill in action;
and the labourers actively engaged in making sugar.
The land on this property and in the region generally,

though of excellent quality, and admirably fitted to the growth of the sugar cane, produces much less sugar than the lands of Jamaica: the canes are less in size, owing to the want of labourers to keep them clean ; and they are renewed by young plants less frequently. Instead of planting cane every three or four years, as in the English colonies, they leave the fields to the rattoon, and gather a scanty harvest from the same plants for ten, twelve, or fifteen years in succession. We saw no plough at work any where. To shew how extremely fertile the soil is, and how much it might be made to produce under good cultivation, the Chief Justice of the Court of Cassation, whose property we next visited, assured us that from two and a half carreaux of virgin land, equal to seven and a half English acres, which he had lately broken up and planted with cane, he had obtained during the first season a quantity of syrup, equal to 60,000 lbs of sugar, or, to thirty hogsheads, of a ton each ! In Jamaica, new cane will sometimes return three hogsheads of sugar per acre, besides rum ; but four hogsheads would be considered an immense harvest. On reaching the habitation of the Chief Justice, we were delighted to find him, like a modern Cincinnatus, in his rustic dress, surrounded, in his large hall, by implements of husbandry, and with the floors of his apartments covered with various field and garden seeds spread out to dry. With a noble air he rose to meet us, gave us a most polite and cordial reception, and entertained us with discourse that was really eloquent. This public functionary is one of the few proprietors who are aiming to improve agriculture by the application of large capital to the soil, and by introducing improvements in every direction. The share system of cultiva-

tion, however, leaves him and the neighbouring proprietors too much dependent on the caprice of their
labourers, whom they are often obliged to allure to hard
work at particular seasons, by the promise of strong
drink! He took us to his distillery and storehouses,
and shewed us, with evident satisfaction, his long
range of vats, filled with rum of different ages, some
of which he tapped for his brother planter, to taste.
At this spot, we learned the following appalling par-
ticulars relative to the consumption of ardent spirit in
Hayti. The great seat of the spirit manufacture in
Hayti is Cayes, as Schedam is in Holland. Here are
manufactured 37,000 barrels of proof spirit yearly. In
the whole island, more than 60,000 barrels are made.
Besides this, there are imported, it is said, 20,000 barrels
from Cuba; but the authorities deny the fact. Taking
the general consumption therefore at only 60,000 barrels
of sixty gallons each, we have an average consumption
of four gallons and a quarter, to every individual of the
whole population! This, it is true, is the only strong
drink of the country, except the wines of France, which
are consumed to some extent in the towns and cities. In
Great Britain and Ireland, each individual, on an average,
consumes more than one gallon of proof spirit, and
half a hogshead of beer, besides cider and wine. Which
of the two countries consumes in proportion the most
alcohol, it would not perhaps be very easy to determine:
both are deeply guilty in this respect; but the practice
of Hayti receives some palliation in the mind of a con-
siderate man, from the circumstance, that its people are
ignorant of the nature of true happiness, and have no
idea in what it consists. Temperance Societies have
been attempted among them; but there being no religious

principle in the land to fall back upon, they fail for
want of support. The want of education, and the
state of the church, and of the army, tend to injure
and demoralize Hayti: ardent spirit is another grand
cause of the national degradation.

On our return to Mocquet, we passed within a
short distance of " La Croix des Bouquets," a village
memorable in the annals of Haytien warfare, the seat of
many a bloody skirmish; and on reaching the plantation found a handsome dinner awaiting us after our
long morning's toil. The planters in these plains have a
supply of delicacies for the table ready at a moment's
notice. Some land turtle were kept secured, by a cord,
tied to the leg of each, in a small pond near the house;
and one of these, and some good fowls, with a variety of
vegetables, rice, and preserved fruits, made us an excellent repast. The evening was delightful when we
remounted our horses to return to Port-au-Prince; but
the sun was soon lost to us, and we passed through
the city-gate in darkness, delighted with our day's
excursion, glad to be at home again, and very weary.
Among the many kind invitations we received, was one
from Senator B. Ardouin, to spend a day or two at his
country villa on the Black Mountain, twenty miles
from the city. We had often heard of *Le Grand fond*
—the awful abyss—the name by which the spot is
designated, on which his house stands; and we accepted
the invitation with much pleasure.

Rarely does it fall to the lot of a traveller, in either
hemisphere, to witness the beauty and grandeur of
natural scenery which met our eye in this memorable
journey. Rising at three o'clock in the morning, we
set out, accompanied by the senator, and three other

gentlemen—six of us in all—attended by two servants.
The waning moon had nearly set, but the stars shone
brightly and lighted our path for many miles, as we
slowly ascended the rough road to Pétionville. This
place was chosen by the government for a second
capital, and the lands around it were sold, and the state
buildings erected with a view to that end, but hitherto
the town has made but little progress. About a mile
further onward, we began the steep ascent of the hills.
As we rose gradually above the plains, grand and
beautiful prospects disclosed themselves on every side :
the city of Port au Prince, with its numerous shipping,
lay at our feet ; on our right hand, was a chain of lofty
hills, green and well wooded ; and on our left, the
extensive plain of the Cul de Sac, sprinkled with
sugar estates, and enlivened by the habitations of
wealthy proprietors. Two large lakes, were conspicuous
in the distance ; and beyond these lay a ridge of mountains that stretched eastward as far as the eye could
reach. Often did we stop to rest, and gaze on the
wonderful scenes around us. Palm trees in great
number, and of extraordinary height and gracefulness,
decorated the mountain sides, and added to the interest
of the foreground. On reaching the top of the black
mountain, the prospect was magnificent. We were now
standing on an eminence six thousand feet above the
plain, just at the point, where, in tropical regions, the
fir and the pine begin to be luxuriant, a forest of which
abounding in trees eighty and a hundred feet in height,
was spread out before us, through which or on its borders
we rode for several miles. The winds agitated the
branches, and occasioned at times a loud cracking and
rustling noise, which so much resembled that of a

river running over a rocky bed, that we looked beyond
and below us, expecting every moment to trace the
rushing waters. At particular passes and bends of the
hills we caught new objects of wonder. From one spot,
we traced the lofty chain of the *La Selle* mountains,
rising abruptly to a further height of twelve or fifteen
hundred feet above our heads ; from another, the island
of Gonave, far away in the ocean ; from a third, the
plain of Jacmel, extending from the foot of the mountains to the sea ; and from a fourth, the hilly country
about St. Mark and Gonaives, nearly a hundred miles
distant by the common road, and which it would have
taken us a three days' journey on horseback to reach !
The laughing woodpecker was running with agility up
the tall trees in search of insects ; and a bird, called the
musician, known only in these regions and rarely seen,
gave out its fine soft notes, like a flute, from the depths
of the woods.

We rode slowly along, enjoying the sights and sounds
of nature, so new and surprising to us, till we came to
Fourcy, the hospitable habitation of our friend the
senator. For the last three miles of this interesting
route, we had come down a gradual descent. The
villa of the plantation stands on a neck of table land,
about 5400 feet above the sea, and is one of the finest
spots imaginable : here we dismounted and formed a
social domestic party for the day. *Fourcy* is a coffee
plantation, worked on shares ; and it was delightful to
see the hearty good-will manifested by the labourers to
their beloved proprietor, who comes but seldom to visit
them, owing to the toil of the ascent, and the numerous
state avocations that detain him in the city. A number
of them clustered round us to take charge of the horses,

and to perform the work of the house during our stay;
a superb *second breakfast* was prepared for us at noon;
after which, we traversed the numerous by-paths that
lead down the sides of the mountains to the dells and
ravines below, and luxuriated, if we may so speak, in
the wonders of creation. The exclamation of Words-
worth's Wanderer, in his address to the author of
Nature, rushed to my recollection.

> " The mind that may forget thee in the crowd,
> Cannot forget thee here, where thou hast built
> For thy own glory in the wilderness!"

The mountains of *La Selle*, which overlook Jacmel
and the sea, were at a distance of six leagues from us,
and between them and the spot where we stood were
profound depths, (des Grands Fonds,) some of them
awfully rugged and rocky, and others filled with forests
of the Weymouth pine; valleys ran between different
ridges of the hills, in which were sprinkled numerous
small properties, neatly fenced, where the owners reside,
and cultivate provisions and coffee. The plantain, the
banana, and the graceful Indian corn, are the products
of the region. The beautiful *Fuchsia*, cultivated as a
green-house plant in some parts of England, is here a
parasite, which clings to the stems of slender trees, and
hangs down its crimson blossoms in rich profusion;
others of our elegant and tender garden plants grow
wild by the road-side. The bay-tree and the ivy, so
common in cold countries, mix with the forest trees
peculiar to a tropical latitude: the standard peach
flourishes and yields good fruit; the apple thrives,
and blackberries of a large size abound: here, in short,
the products of the old and the new world blend
together in strange luxuriance, and exhibit a vegetation

remarkable in appearance and extraordinary for its richness and beauty. The thermometer ranged in the day time from 60° to 64° of Fahrenheit; and the evening and early morning were so chilly as to render a cloak or some other warm clothing necessary. The dinner table was abundantly supplied with soup, fish, fowl, ragouts, and roasted meat; numerous fine vegetables, tarts, creams, and confectionary, and a rich dessert; coffee concluded the day. Our hospitable host showed the kindest attention to his guests; such attentions as genuine courtesy dictates, and true politeness knows how to apply; and entertained and instructed us by conversation of no common order. The senator Ardouin is a travelled gentleman, who went a few years since on a mission to the court of France, and paid a hasty visit to England on his return home.

The next morning our party, some on foot, and others on horseback, went down a steep hill to visit the fields of one of the new small proprietors settled in this district. The estate in question was purchased nine years ago, and consists of twenty-seven acres of good land, part of it in well-pruned young coffee trees, which the owner cultivates with the assistance of his son-in-law, wife, and daughters. The dwellings for the two separate families are neat and comfortable, and very well furnished; their coffee is clean and vigorous, their gardens are flourishing, their fences neat—every thing indicating order, industry, and content. All the inmates, parents and children, were uneducated, and evidently superstitious; with this exception, their condition seemed an enviable one. Could we have relied on the condition of these families as being a fair specimen of the rural peasantry of Hayti, we should have said that education and the spread of gospel truth only, were needed to make this land one of the finest on the face of the globe; not only lovely in its natural features, but in the contentment and genuine happiness of its people. Some of the old mountain estates are fast declining; in part because the coffee trees begin to wear out, and to leave the land in what is called *ruinate;* and partly because the former labourers desert them, and buy new land for themselves.

On *Fourcy*, there were, not long since, thirty-two cultivators; there are now but twelve: the remainder have abandoned it, and have become freeholders in their own right. Under Toussaint, no person was allowed to buy less than fifty carreaux, or 150 acres of land ; under the present government, the quantity purchaseable of the State is reduced to five carreaux, or fifteen acres, and this may be obtained at so moderate a price, as to be within the reach of every healthy industrious man. Owing to the cheapness of good land, the labourers, who work for hire, already reduced in number by the civil wars, are now still further diminished ; and a proprietor, if he wish to secure the services of those who have long laboured for him on the moiety system, must be content to allow them even greater advantages than that system affords. The few remaining labourers on *Fourcy* not only take their half of the 10,000 lbs of coffee which the plantation yields, but appropriate to themselves almost the whole of the provisions which the land furnishes, sending down only a few of the rarer vegetables, beans, peas, and artichokes, to their master, for his table at Port-au-Prince, and supplying his need when he comes to reside for a few days in the country. This he knows very well, but has no alternative, but to bear it quietly.

After a second mid-day repast, our little company
began its downward march to the plain of Port-au-
Prince. On returning we rested at Petionville, and
received entertainment at the house of a public functionary
who accommodates strangers, but who refused to receive
anything from us as a return for his civilities. We
reached the city as the sun was setting in its usual
splendour behind the hills. Whoever wishes to gratify
himself with some of the finest scenery in Hayti, should
ascend the mountain we had just traversed, and explore
the region of *Le Grand Fond*, and the stupendous
heights of *La Selle*. The roads on this route are every
where good; the passes in some places are steep and
rocky, but affording, as they do, a firm foot-hold to the
horses, are no where dangerous.

Our next journey was a much longer one, and something painful in its character, from the fatigues to which
it subjected us. It was our wish to visit Jacmel, and
the southern coast, by the way of Leogane, the principal town of the arrondissement commanded by General
Inginac, whose passport was needful to us. On making
the General a call to solicit his leave to travel, he
replied in the kindest manner—" You may travel anywhere; the President was well satisfied with the interview
you had with him, and it is our wish to make your stay
in the country as agreeable as possible. When is it your
wish to set out ?" On mentioning the day, he continued,.
" The journey is too long for Madame on horseback ; if
she exerts herself in this manner, she will take fever ; you
must go across the level country in a carriage, and take
to your horses when you reach the mountain road. Fix
the hour of departure, and I will send you a carriage,
horses, and postilion, and one of the clerks from my

office shall accompany you as far as my sugar estate at the bottom of the mountain, where you shall sup and lodge." Early in the morning, long before sunrise, the General's private carriage, with two horses and a hand-some mule, all abreast, and a servant in military uniform came up to the gate of our lodging house. We presently seated ourselves and drove off, at the rate of seven or eight miles an hour, over a tolerably good road, running part of the way through a mangrove swamp by the sea-side. At the distance of sixteen miles, we halted at a sugar estate belonging to the General's family, and waited for a change of horses, which his clerk had rode forward to procure : he had to search them on a neighbouring property, which detained us nearly an hour, but this circumstance gave us the opportunity of observing the nature of the surrounding country which in this part of the island is an extensive pasture of fine short grass, on which herds of cattle are kept to graze, and which is intersected by newly enclosed fields, where sugar is cultivated. The mango and other trees were growing at random, singly or in groups, about the different properties; and only a few houses could be seen. Another hour's travel, of six or eight miles, brought us to Leogane. Our attendant, the man of office, girded after the manner of the country with a long sword, took us to the house of a maiden lady, sister of the General, who had received from him a previous intimation of our coming. Here we found a breakfast prepared for us of cutlets, stewed fowl, plantains, red pottage, and coffee, and we were waited upon by the Colonel-com-mandant and Captain of the station, who expressed a wish to gratify us in everything we desired to see.

Leogane is a small town containing about three thousand inhabitants, standing on a park-like plain, within a mile of the sea-shore; the roads in the neighbourhood are good, and in some places well shaded by trees; but the streets are exceedingly dull, showing nothing of the bustle of commerce. The military alone enliven the place, and give it a temporary consequence. Again setting out, we passed over a district of land covered with green turf, as short and beautiful as the well-kept lawn of an English mansion, and, in about an hour, we reached the spot where we were invited to pitch our tent for the night. We took advantage of the little remaining day-light to survey the rural establishment. The name of this property is Dufort: it has about thirty-six acres of land in sugar cane, and manufactures 240 barrels of tafia per annum, of the value altogether of about £1300. sterling; and the pastures are fed off by sheep and cattle. The estate, like most others in this part of the country, is worked on the share system. The proprietor pays himself five per cent. for the use of machinery, together with all the expenses of management and restores the oxen and horses that have died during the year or which have grown too old to work. What remains in value of the produce after satisfying these demands is divided equally between the proprietor and the labourers, leaving the latter in most instances, but a small sum for each; but then they pay no rent, are allowed pasture for their horses, keep pigs, goats, and poultry, gather fruit from the trees, and raise their own provisions on grounds set apart for their use. At the time of our visit the sugar mill was at work, and the place was full of bustle and gaiety.

In Jamaica the sugar mills are generally worked by wind, water, or steam; in this country, they are

worked by horses, the horses being attached to the circumference of a large wheel; driven round with a long
whip, by a man who sits on one of the naves that
project from a huge shaft in the centre : the poor animals
are made to go very quick, and seem to be used with
very little mercy. Men, women, and children, were all
employed in some one or other of the operations attendant
on the manufacture of tafia, which is here found to be a
more profitable direction of capital than the crystalliza-
tion of the syrup into sugar. The labourers' provision
grounds, and the gardens attached to the homestall, were
in good order, and yielded an abundant supply of the
common necessaries of life. As we were walking over
the farm we came to a hilly spot, on which were
browzing what looked like a flock of goats, but on a
nearer approach, we discovered them to be sheep; and
such sheep as we had never seen before : hair instead of
wool covered their backs, and they were all either spotted
or ringstraked ! They were probably, in kind and appearance, the very counterpart of that portion of Laban's
flock, which formed the wages and patrimony of the
patriarch Jacob ; and if sheep and goats, in ancient time,
had as near a resemblance to each other, as this kind
of sheep bears to the goats of our own country, we may
see at once the peculiar force of our Lord's words in
reference to the end of the world, as intimating some
skill and discernment on the part of the shepherd, whose
province it is to divide the flocks :—" Before Him shall
be gathered all nations: and He shall separate them one
from another, as a shepherd divideth his sheep from the
goats." The flock of sheep on this estate was perfectly
unique in its character : we met with none such anywhere else ; the ground of the skin and hair was white,

the spots and rings were dark-brown : they were spotted
like leopards, or striped like the zebra.

Very early the next morning our whole establishment
was in motion : our saddle horses from Port-au-Prince
had arrived in the evening, together with an ass for the
baggage, and two guides to conduct us over the mountains. The horses were brought out to be saddled for
the journey ; the postilion was busy in fixing his team
to the empty carriage ; servants were engaged in preparing us coffee, or in assisting to load the poor ass with
his panniers ; and there was much clatter, and some
little confusion, before we got fairly under weigh. The
clerk from the General's office still kept us company ;
having received instructions not to leave us till we
should reach the summit of the mountain, 5000 feet
above the plain ; and till we should have the port of
Jacmel full in view. Very slow and toilsome was our
upward march by star-light ; now through the shade
of thick trees that covered the road with their branches,
and now along a river course that swept among the hills,
and which it was impossible to avoid crossing many
times during the journey. The air was delightfully
cool till a little after sun-rise, when the heat, notwithstanding the very high ground we were traversing, began
to be oppressive : after six hours of hard toil we reached
the summit. It would be difficult to a person not
acquainted with mountain scenery in the tropics to form
a conception of the grandeur and loveliness of nature, as
exhibited in these wonderful hills. Jamaica and Martinique have scenes surpassing fable, but Hayti has
prospects more beautiful, and is richer still. At many
points everything but high hills and deep valleys is
shut out from view : the hills in many places, to a con-

siderable extent, being covered with timber trees, the
growth   perhaps   of   centuries,   interspersed   with   the
graceful   cabbage   palm,—the   tree   of   liberty,   which   is
cultivated   and   fostered   as   the   emblem   of   national
freedom :   the   valleys   and   low   rising   ground   being
sprinkled   with   neat   well   fenced   cottages,   green   with
Indian   corn   and   the   broad   leafed   banana,   or   covered
with   numerous   patches   of   the   white   flowering   coffee!
The people of Hayti, if they display no other refine-
ment,   shew   admirable   taste   in   the   choice   of   place   and
situation   to   live   in :   some   of   the   sweetest   spots   in
creation   are   covered   with   their   dwellings,   where   to   all
appearance   at   least,   they   live   a   peaceful,   contented,
and   happy   life.   Were   such   a   land   as   this   colonized
by   Europeans,   we   should   hear   no   end   of   its   praise.
Our   kind   host   the   General's   bailiff,   in   the   valley
below,   had   furnished   us   with   ample   provision   in   the
shape   of   mutton ;   and   a   cottager   at   the   spot   where   we
rested,   boiled   us   some   coffee   and   cooked   some   eggs,
on which we made a noon-day repast : while the horses
which   the   guides   had   tethered,   feasted   on   bundles   of
juicy guinea grass.   Superstition, standing in the place
of religion, spreads its influence over hill and dale : the
mountain   top   and   the   lowest   valley   equally   feel   its
prevailing power.   In this remote spot, which the parish
priest,   in   his   rounds   but   seldom   visits,   we   discovered   a
household   altar   dedicated   to   the   Virgin,   and   strewed
with crosses, where the poor devotees of the little settle-
ment repair to pay their devotions.   A page or two of
a missal or some Romish legend, which probably none
could   read,   were   placed   in   due   order   on   a   table   before
the   crucifix!   heathenism   and   popery   are   unhappily
blended in this benighted land, and keep the people in

chains of ignorance and fear. How animating is the
consideration that a better state of things is destined,
sooner or later, to gladden the earth! The evangelical prophet says in speaking of the reign of the
Messiah, that "he shall not fail nor be discouraged till
he have set judgment in the earth, and the isles shall
wait for his law." Hayti is undoubtedly one of the
islands comprehended in this cheering declaration; and
it is surely the duty of professing Christians, who
behold her miserable state to stretch out a hand to
help her.

After we had well rested, we began to descend towards
the plains on the southern coast. Our attendant here
took leave of us: one of our guides lagged behind with
the ass and panniers; and, with the other guide on
foot, we now pursued our journey alone. The views
were most extensive and transcendently fine: on one
side, we could trace the ocean shore northward, almost
to Cape Nicholas Mole, a hundred and fifty miles
distant; on another, there rose the towering heights
of *La Selle*, extending in an interminable range towards
the east; and below us, twenty miles off, apparently
embosomed in woods, lay the town of Jacmel, which
though so distant from the spot where we stood, appeared
so near that a schoolboy would have said he could sling
a stone into it. The steeps and declivities of our downward path were fearful; but the horses kept their feet
firmly, and we received no harm.

In one part of the road, we passed through a grove of
Seville orange trees loaded with ripe fruit, but unpalatable
to us, though we needed refreshment. On coming near
to the bottom of the mountains, the scenery assumed
something of an English aspect; and but for tropical trees,

so unlike any thing European, we might have imagined ourselves in Derbyshire. The broad smooth river, and the bold rocks, which from their vast and irregular layers, seem to have been heaved up by some violent concussion, were singularly picturesque and beautiful. Had not excessive fatigue weighed down our spirits and depressed our energies, we should hardly have known how to admire the scenery enough ; but the horses were jaded, and would scarcely do more than move, even with the whip. We had many miles yet to travel ; and both of us had become faint for want of refreshment, which however we obtained in an unexpected manner. My wife discovered a guava tree loaded with ripe fruit, and stopped her horse to gather some. The fruit was fine and juicy, and both cheered and invigorated us : the effects it produced reminded us of the honey which Jonathan discovered in the wood ; " he put forth the end of the rod that was in his hand, and dipped it in an honeycomb, and put his hand to his mouth : and his eyes were enlightened." Our horses stopped to drink of the river, and to snatch some juicy leaves ; and we then passed slowly along, often outstripped by our guide on foot, till we reached our wished for destination, in a comfortable boarding-house at Jacmel. The day's journey had been thirty miles; in performing which, we had been eleven hours on horseback, except as we occasionally dismounted to avoid the danger of steep declivities, and to relieve the horses.

Our first visitor at Jacmel was a mulatto gentlewoman, the widow of a black man, who had filled the office of Collector of the Customs ; and who occupied one of the best houses in the place. She had lived in the United States, and spoke our language fluently ; and came to pay us respect as strangers. This kind-hearted matron paid us several visits, furnished us with sweet cakes and fruit, entertained us at her table, and introduced us to some of the best families of the place. Her conduct was the more remarkable, as, in America, she had suffered grievous persecution from the cruel prejudice existing in that country against colour. Her first husband was a sea-captain : on one occasion, she left the shore with him in the boat, to take a final leave of him on board the vessel, and was carried by the winds to a greater distance from home than she expected. The boat re-conveyed her to the shore and landed her at a strange place. Seeing a tavern, she made her way to it to obtain lodging for the night : the landlady looked at her repulsively, and spurned her from the door. " We take in no niggers here," was her coarse language ; " if you want to rest, go to the nigger huts on the top of the hill !" The poor lady told us her heart was too full to bear this unchristian rebuke with meekness : she sat down and burst into tears. She did, however, toil up to the negro's huts, and was there received kindly.

The Americans, in their own estimation and boast, are the freest people on the face of the globe : according to the terms of their constitution, " all men are free and equal ;" yet they treat the houseless stranger, if tinged with a coloured skin, as one of nature's outcasts ! Whenever a white man from America or Europe falls sick in Jacmel, no one is so ready to offer to nurse him and shew him kindness, as this poor despised woman, whose mother was an African. What a contrast ; and what a striking lesson does such a fact as this teach to the proud republicans of " Columbia's happy land !" The son and son-in-law of General Inginac, Secretary of

State for Hayti, on their return home a few years since
from Paris, where they had been received in a manner
suited to their rank and station in life, landed at New
York, with a view of visiting the United States; but
no tavern or boarding-house keeper, would receive them
as guests, for fear of giving offence to the inhabitants of
that city!

One of the richest merchants at Port-au-Prince,
whose father was one of Christophe's barons, assured
me that he went into a woollen draper's store in Phila-
delphia, and desiring to be measured for a black coat,
the storekeeper retorted with an impudent falsehood,
" We have no cloth here, sir:" a hatter also, whose store
was attended, when he called, by some white customers,
refused to sell him a hat! Such is the tyranny of
public opinion in this professedly free land, that a man
dare not protest against conduct like this, and call it
as it is, barbarous and unchristian, without the danger
of being treated contemptuously. The Haytiens have
a settled dislike against the Americans, owing to this
deep rooted and wicked prejudice, which the latter
carry so far as to refuse to admit any Haytien citizen
to act in their ports as a Consul for his own nation.
But the subject is too sickening to dwell upon.

The town of Jacmel consists of two parts; the lower
town, built along the shore at the bottom of a bay
where the shipping lies, and where business is carried
on ; and the upper town, built on a hill immediately
behind the lower. The view of this port from a ship's
deck at sea with its white buildings and terrace-like
form, must be very striking. The streets are poor and
ill-paved ; and there are not many good houses : the
best building in the place belongs to the President,

who is seldom there, and which therefore stands empty.
The inhabitants are estimated at from six to seven thousand. There is a good market place; a spacious, and
rather handsome, parish church; and a strong prison.
A ship from Havre, and a fine brig bound for Liverpool,
were taking in cargoes of coffee and logwood; and a
considerable number of coasting sloops lay at anchor in
the harbour. The beach extends nearly the whole
length of the bay, and forms a delightful promenade.
We often walked there to enjoy the sea-breezes, and to
survey the amphitheatre of fine hills that enclose the
town.

A kind of nautilus called the *Portuguese man-of-war*
which spreads a sail to the wind, and floats on the
wave, is very abundant in this part of the ocean : whole
fleets of this species of jelly fish are sometimes driven on
the shore : early one morning we found a multitude of
them alive on the beach, every one of them clinging
with its tentacula to some stone or shell, as if to avoid
being swept back again to the angry surge. If touched
with the naked hand, they inflict a sharp sting, like
other animals of the mollusca tribe : so that in order to
examine them minutely, you are compelled to take them
up carefully between two pieces of wood. The body of
the animal is firm and transparent, and reflects like a
prism, the bright colours of the rainbow : its form when
narrowly scrutinized, is more intelligible than appears at
first view : its head and eyes are distinctly visible, and a
broad margin of fringe beautifully gay with red and
violet, which we supposed it might sometimes spread
for a sail, is attached to its side. The arteries of the
body, and the muscles that move this fringe may be
clearly traced : its tentacula are numerous; but instead

of being white, as they appear to be when under water,
they exhibit the same varied colours as the body, only
somewhat of a darker and deeper hue. This animal
does not, as some have supposed, inhabit the shell of
the nautilus, but is of a totally distinct tribe—distinct
both in appearance, and in its manner and habits of life.
Shell fish of different species are sometimes swept on
these shores; but we saw none of any value or beauty
during our stay.

Among the families which we visited at Jacmel
was that of the procureur, or state attorney of the
district, whom we had met at Port au Prince, and who
politely invited us to a second breakfast; four servants
waited at table, but all of them sat down on a chair,
when not engaged in attending to the wants of the company. This family was a highly interesting group: well
informed, and of polished manners; and had more of a
Christian bearing than is common in this country. The
French Bible, without comment, was lying on the table,
and one of the sons told me it was their constant practice,
though Roman Catholics, to read a portion of it every
morning, before they entered on the business and duties of
the day. There was a good library in the house. The
public school of Jacmel is conducted on the monitorial
system, under the care of an accomplished black man,
who has about seventy scholars. There are also three
private schools, where about 120 boys and girls are
educated. The prison disappointed me, being very
narrow and confined, and grievously inadequate to its
purpose : there is but one small day-yard for men and
women, tried and untried, old and young, sane and
insane ! The soldiers, who sit as sentries at the gates of
these prisons, lolling and smoking their cigars, sometimes

assume the most amusing consequence : one of them, on our entering the court, insisted on searching my hat to see whether any knife or sharp instrument were concealed there for any of the prisoners, and justified his rudeness on the plea of duty.

The prisoners here, as in other places, are allowed only a single gourdine, or five pence sterling per week, for food. A captain and three soldiers under arms, together with the jailer, attended us through the different apartments. One great cause of crime in this district is, the free consumption of rum and tafia. The chief clerk of the customs informed me that from 1800 to 2000 barrels were landed here every year, for use in the town and neighbourhood; this would give to 30,000 inhabitants, the number residing in the arrondissement, an average of four gallons to each individual; but as many of the small proprietors carry their coffee to market at Cayes, and return loaded with spirits by land carriage, the quantity consumed is much greater. The calculation founded on an estimate given me by our Vice-Consul at Port-au-Prince, makes the quantity five gallons and a half to each individual! There is now no British Consul at Jacmel : the last gentleman who filled this office, James Hodges, an English merchant, left the island a few years since, and has left behind him the regrets and good wishes of all classes of the inhabitants. Our country had in him an upright able representative, whose loss will not easily be repaired.

After spending a week in this district, we prepared to return to the capital, having engaged a servant on mule-back to convey our baggage, and act as our guide. We were no sooner mounted and ready to start, than the guide attempted to mount his mule, which became

intolerably restive, and refused to stir a step forward :
it kicked violently, and threw off the panniers; so
that our provisions prepared for the journey were scattered in the open street.   From this untoward circumstance, it was so late, before we cleared the town, that
instead of journeying as we had intended, in the cool
early morning, the sun soon rose upon us and shed his
fierce beams on our heads.   We stopped to breakfast at
a negro cabin by the roadside, but speedily resumed our
route.   Our pathway in this direction lay in the course
of the river Jacmel, which rises high in the mountains,
and pours down in the rainy season an immense body
of water to the sea : we crossed the bed of this river
more than sixty times, till one of the horses became so
jaded and weary with the fording, that we were obliged
to dismount, and to lead the poor animal along in the
best manner we could, up the steep hills and along the
mountain precipices; and we should ourselves have been
worn out with the toil and anxiety, had we not been
rewarded with such magnificent scenery in every direction, as more than compensated for all our pains and
trouble.   At two o'clock, P. M., having journeyed
twenty-four miles, we reached a coffee habitation on
the declivity of the Gros Morne, where the good people
took us in, cut grass for the horses, and provided us with
coffee, and a good bed.   The master of the house was
the overseer of the plantation, which he cultivated on
the share system, he was surrounded by numerous fellow-
labourers, whose decent cabins were scattered in the
most picturesque manner among the neighbouring hills ;
and who here went by the name of *cultivators.*

We no where observed in Hayti, those terraced flat
pavements so common in Jamaica, under the name of

barbacues, where planters spread out their coffee to prepare for pulping, and where the pulped berry is left to dry in the sun.   All the operations for which a barbacue serves elsewhere are performed in Hayti on the naked ground, in the open air; hence the coffee, which in this country has a peculiarly fine aromatic flavour, gets mixed with particles of grit and dirt, which adds to the weight and deteriorates the quality, and greatly lessens its value in the foreign market. In some municipalities, where coffee is brought to market, the bags are narrowly examined to ascertain what portion of dirt they contain; and the mayor of one town assured us, that his regulations were so strict on this head, that parties disposed to practice deceit met with summary punishment. This neglect of cleanliness in the dressing of coffee is one proof, among many others, of the natural indolence of the people: naked children are suffered to roam about at pleasure, who might be trained to the useful work of picking out the dirty particles, and by the increased value thus given to the commodity, might provide themselves with an abundance of good clothing. A semi-civilized people will always continue to tread in the beaten path of those who have gone before them, caring to turn neither to the right hand nor the left, whatever profit or advantage a change of path might bring; indolence benumbs, and ignorance blinds them.   Such is Hayti at the present moment, and such it will be till education raises it from its sunken level.

Early the next morning, my wife on horseback, myself and the guide on foot, again set forward, and in about two hours reached the summit of Gros Morne. It is impossible by any description to convey a picture of

the fine panorama which here burst on our view in all its
extent, and with its splendour of tropical scenery—the
wide ocean, the lofty hills, the extensive plain, the broad
river course, and the far distant mountains. Our guide
assured us, that from this very spot he had often on a
clear day, seen as far as Cape Nicholas Mole, on the
north-west of the island; nearly a hundred and fifty
miles distant! The passage in this direction over Gros
Morne, which is here about 5000 feet in height, is one of
great interest, not only from the vast outlines of nature,
but from the extraordinary fruitfulness and loveliness of
the foreground, and from the numerous houses and small
villages that adorn it. On descending the mountain
towards the plain of Leogane, we passed by a hedge of
white jessamine in full flower; and saw pine apples
growing under the trees. On reaching the level ground,
we stopped at a solitary house, belonging to a sugar
property, to breakfast and take rest. The hut, for such
we must call it, was one of the common negro houses
in which slaves formerly resided: it consisted of two
apartments, one fitted up as a sleeping-room, the other
serving as a day-room for all purposes, giving ingress
and egress to human beings, fowls, goats, sheep, and
pigs! It contained a table, a stool, and two or three
chairs, and a fire was lighted at the far end, where the
mistress of the family was cooking her pottage. Several
men were sauntering about as if they had nothing to do,
and could live without work; a naked boy kept watch
and ward at the door-way to keep the pigs from molest-
ing us, and we patiently sat down to take such a
survey of common life as the curious scene afforded us.
Presently, a pet lamb made its appearance; when the
boy left his post, and hugging it with delight, took it to

his grandmother, who sat at the porridge pot, and who
fed it with the peelings of some sweet potatoes which
she was preparing for a savory mess. Extreme rudeness
and ignorance characterized all around us ; and when
we had seen enough we departed. Here we hired a
mule, to relieve our jaded sick horse, which the guide
attached by a cord to his own mule, and suffered to
trot or walk as it pleased. There are numerous sugar
estates in this part of the plain, through several of
which we passed; they contained a numerous population, but many of the men and women were meanly
clad, and some of the great boys and girls were in a
state of perfect nudity,

Grecié is a village by the side of the road, leading
from Leogane to the capital, about fifteen miles distant
from the latter, and here finding a good tavern and
excellent accommodations, we stopped to dine and
lodge. In the course of the evening we walked out to
visit some of the habitations close by, and were much
interested in a provision ground, cultivated as a market
garden, in the less common kind of vegetables, such as
green peas, butter-beans, tomatoes, and the sweet
potato : the proprietor had led down a water course
from the hills in such a manner, as to give it irrigation
in every part, and a fine crop was the result and reward
of his diligence. In the morning our journey recom-
menced, and at ten o'clock, we arrived safely, once more,
at Port-au-Prince.

CHAPTER VIII.

THE FINE ARTS — PHYSIOGNOMY OF THE NATIVES —
INEFFICIENCY OF THE CITY POLICE — DEPARTURE
FROM HAYTI — CONCLUDING OBSERVATIONS.

THE descendants of Africa may be said to excel in the
imitative arts; the boys at school write in general a
superior hand, and succeed well in those branches of
business which are purely mechanical, and require no
exercise of the higher powers of the mind; but neither
in Hayti, nor in any other nation of the African race, is
civilization so far advanced as to lead us to look for the
efforts of genius in the cultivation of the fine arts.
There are in this country a few artists by profession,
who obtain a living by portrait painting; and there is
one at Cape Haytien who excels in the higher branches
of the profession, and has produced pictures which are
likely to give him a name. The portraits we saw in
different houses were, in general, a tame coloured map of
the human face, very like the original in the contour and
common features, but without a particle of life or spirit;
just such resemblances as pass in this country under the
name of *wooden*. Pictures of this sort are very numerous, and stare you in the face in houses of an inferior
description, where you would little expect to see them.
Vanity is common to the human mind; and it cannot be
expected that unlettered negroes should be free from it.
The next sort of pictures in common demand are *holy
families*, copied from the old masters, saints at prayer,
and allegorical representations of angels in heaven; of

these we saw some good specimens from the hands
of Dejoie, a native artist, which give an idea to the
observer of what, under good instruction, and by
studying the old masters, he might become capable of
performing. His great work, which is placed in the
senate house at Port-au-Prince, is the historical picture
of the entry of President Boyer and his generals into
the city of Cape Haytien, soon after the death of
Christophe; the grouping is spirited, the portraits are
good, and the execution altogether is highly creditable
to his taste and skill. We visited the store-shop of an
artist, to look over his collection of views of the city
and port, which we found very hard and meagre;
some copied portraits interested us greatly—Pétion,
Christophe, Dessalines, and others. That of Dessalines,
in his scarlet uniform, we should suppose, from his
known character, to be true to the original, fierce,
ignorant, and cruel—the picture of a chief, who, as
the Haytiens say of him, " never spared a man in his
anger," and who was remorseless in all his doings.
Christophe has a milder countenance, with the bearing
of a gentleman; and the portrait of Pétion is every
way pleasing in its expression.

Alexander Pétion, the first President of the republic
of Hayti, was perhaps less beloved in his life-time, than
his memory has been venerated since his death. High
mass every year is said for his departed soul with great
pomp and circumstance, according to the rites of the
Romish church; and the people appear to look back
upon him with more than a common feeling of kindness
and regard, as the father and friend of his country.
There is an engraved bust of him with an inscription,
which may be considered an echo of the public senti-

ment. " Il n'a jamais fait couler larmes à personne, sauf
à sa mort."* The body of this chief encased in a coffin,
lies in an open cenotaph fronting the government house,
and by the side of it, that of his only daughter : both
coffins are occasionally decorated with simple votive
offerings : a picture of the Virgin and a cross are placed
on a pedestal behind the coffins, to arrest and elevate the
devotions of the faithful. There is no doubt that Pétion
was a patriot, and that he sincerely desired the welfare
of Hayti : he was greatly averse to the shedding of
blood, and had often to check the impetuosity and
vengeance of the generals who commanded under him.
Some accounts represent him to have starved himself
to death through vexation at the slow progress of his
people towards civilisation ; this might have been the
case, as he was of a sanguine temperament, and was
exceedingly thwarted in some of his plans for the public
good : but a physician of Port-au-Prince assured me
that such was not really the fact, and that he died of
inanition from natural causes. President Boyer, makes
it his boast that he treads in the steps of his illustrious
predecessor : he has lately signified his wish to the
house of representatives, that a statue in marble may be
erected to his memory. I do not remember to have
seen a single statue, public or private in Hayti ; and
there is probably no artist in the island capable of producing one : nor is there a single edifice that indicates
genius in the mind of the architect ; all is coarse or
common. There is nothing to be lamented in this ;
conveniences, not luxuries, are the wants of a republic,
and so long as these are attended to in the spirit of an

---

* He never caused the tears of any one to flow but when he died.

improving age, it is all that the friends of good order
can for a long time wish for, or need be at all anxious
to promote. A large number of the mulatto class of citizens
residing at the capital, came over as emigrants from the
United States, and are distinct in their physiognomy
from the Creoles; their countenance in general is rather
coarse and forbidding, whereas the native mulattos,
especially the women, have a softness and subdued
expression that is very pleasing. Perhaps it is that
the features become more agreeable in proportion as
a people recede from the effects and influence of slavery.
It is rather a remarkable fact, that out of the sixty or
seventy Romish priests now officiating in the island, one
only is a coloured man; although many of the brown
people are well taught in the public schools, and some of
them are more than on a par, in point of scholarship and
manners, with the rude priests imported from Corsica.
The priests from Europe have succeeded in keeping the
common people in bonds of the grossest superstition,
and have made them believe, to adopt a phrase in common use, well understood by the vulgar, *that coloured
baptism will not stick!* All the dollars received from
baptisms are wanted for the pockets of white men,
exclusively. There are some superstitions, which as not
affecting materially the income of the priests, are left
untouched and unreproved; the burial of poor people
without the rites of the church is one of them: the
choir and the crucifix are unsought for because there is
no money to pay for them; but to bury without rites
of any kind, is repugnant to their feelings; hence,
heathen ceremonies are commonly resorted to; libations
are poured out, and a table is spread for the dead, of

common eatables, very much after the manner of the Chaldeans, as represented in the apocryphal story of Bel and the Dragon. It sometimes happens that people, who possess money enough to pay the priest for a handsome interment, prefer the practice of heathen ceremonies, from the habits and associations to which they have been long accustomed. How much are public schools and christian instruction needed in this dark land!

We heard much, during our stay at Port-au-Prince of the extreme inefficiency of the police: crimes of a deep dye are not often perpetrated, but when they do occur, they seem to excite but little attention; and the criminal, if a determined active man, will sometimes elude pursuit. During our stay at Port-au-Prince, a murder was committed within a few doors of our own lodgings; a wicked fellow who had masked his face for the carnival, went into the house of an American emigrant, and attempted to take hold of his daughter; the father strove to prevent him; a scuffle ensued, the girl ran between them to part the combatants, when the murderer drew out a dagger, and stabbed her to the heart. The military guard was immediately informed of the fact; the murderer was known, but escaped. It was only an American girl that lost her life, and so the matter ended! With a large standing army of soldiers who do nothing, how disgraceful are facts like these! An efficient *civil* police is greatly needed in the large towns.

Towards the close of our sojourn at the capital, and before we left the country, we accepted an invitation from the missionary Hartwell, to spend a few days in his family; he and his wife, had but lately arrived from England, and we took the opportunity of exploring the city, and making our inquiries and observations together. We shall long remember their kindness and affection towards us, and the very pleasant hours we spent, both in their society, and in that of the small Christian band, in whose religious welfare they feel so deep an interest. The brig, *Henry Delafield*, bound to New York, was lying in the harbour, when we returned from Jacmel : by this vessel we engaged a passage, and agreed to set sail for that port. Our residence in Hayti was rather more than three months.

The reader will perceive that nothing has been said of the eastern or Spanish part of the island ; our travels were confined to the western or French part ; and it was my wish to speak only from actual observation of what we saw and heard on the spot. It now remains for us only, in conclusion, to take a view of the general state of the country, of the causes of its present degradation, and of the means by which it may be happily raised to its proper rank in the scale of nations.

The causes of the degradation of Hayti being numerous, many agencies must be called into operation, in order to effect the desired change in her condition. The dense ignorance of her population,—their intemperate use of ardent spirits,—the large size, and the mal-administration of the standing army, and the corruptions of the Church, are the great antagonist forces against which an advancing civilization must long have to contend. How are these forces to be resisted ? How are these elements of evil to be overcome ? The grand remedy for the ignorance that prevails, is obvious : it is to establish schools in the country towns and villages, and to encourage elementary education. The government of the country, which professes to feel a deep interest in the spread of knowledge, devotes at present only the very small and insignificant sum of £1000 sterling per annum, towards the support of public schools ; and these schools are for boys only, and exist but in six or seven of the larger towns. The republic, it must be confessed, is crippled for want of funds, and cannot extend farther aid in this department without great economy, and extensive retrenchments. But are the rulers of Hayti prepared to pursue such a course, as the present state of society demands? To a certain extent, we trust, they are ; as since the preceding pages were written, information has reached this country, that the good work of amelioration has been already begun, and that a reduction in the numerical force of the army, to the extent of one-third, has been decreed by the legislature. This measure, the beginning of a great change in the policy of the country, inspires us with much hope for the future ; although in an economical point of view, nothing is yet gained by it for the cause of education; since the money saved by disbanding one-third of the army is to be applied to the increasing of the pay of the two-thirds that remain. Reform, however, has fairly begun its course; the wedge has entered at the right place, and a few continued strokes, judiciously given, may drive it farther and farther, till the army is nearly, if not entirely broken up. The same power which has reduced it from twenty-four thousand men to sixteen thousand, may soon, if it please, put an end to it altogether. It is to this disbanding of the army, as the chief source of saving, in conjunction with measures for regulating the custom-house duties, and for restoring the currency to a sound and healthy state, that

Hayti must look for pecuniary means to carry forward the work of education. This point obtained, all other difficulties may be speedily overcome. The island is at present divided and sub-divided into military districts, and the same mode of division, probably with very little change, might be adopted as the basis of an exten-sive school organization. When colleges succeed to camps, and country school-rooms to the village guard-house, an immense benefit will accrue to the population at large. The Romish priests of the island are opposed to the enlightenment of the common people, as might naturally be expected, and their influence, to a certain extent, will be exerted against it; but the power of this class of functionaries, to obstruct the spread of know-ledge, is happily less here than in most other parts of the world. " Put me, I pray thee, into one of the priest's offices, that I may eat a piece of bread," is, in substance, the petition to the President of Hayti, of almost every ecclesiastic who sets his foot on the soil : the President, and not the Pope, is the head of the Church, and it is too much to suppose, that the hatred of the priests to the spread of knowledge, should lead them to oppose their own temporal interests,—the very interests which, above all others, it is the chief study of their lives to promote and secure. Should any one of them prove refractory on the point of education, and attempt to thwart the measures of the Government, the President has power to *translate* him from a richer living to a poorer one; or if it should please him to do so, he may banish him from the country altogether. The system of instruction to be looked to, as most in harmony with the existing arrangements of the country, is that of the British and Foreign School Society, which extends tuition to both sexes,—which excludes creeds and catechisms, and which encourages the use of the Bible, as a class-book. This system is already in operation at Cape Haytien, and may easily be made to accommodate itself to the feelings and wants of the people in all other places. The Lyceum at Port au Prince, already a Normal school, and a very effective one, is well fitted for the training of young men, to carry out the monitorial plan of teaching; and would, in a few years, furnish a sufficient number of masters for the whole island, more especially if good salaries were offered them, and if the appointment of school-master were made an honorable one, by the express patronage of the President. As there is now no jealousy in Hayti of foreign philanthropic interference, and as the character of England stands high with its people, the friends of education in this country have it in their power, at the present moment, to render the republic an essential service by opening a correspondence with its chief, and by offering to furnish, or to assist in furnishing, elementary books, maps, charts, globes, and other school materials. A liberal encouragement of this sort, in the beginning of such a laudable enterprise, would probably effect much good. Any approach, on our part, to a friendly understanding with the rulers of Hayti, on the subject of education, would be received in the kindest manner; our motives would be correctly appreciated, and the suggestions made by us, would, in all probability, obtain their deliberate and serious consideration. A system of national education, wisely conceived, and rightly applied, is the grand moral desideratum for the

country. We have stated, in the course of the foregoing
narrative, that the people in general are of slothful
habits. Idleness is a vice inherent in all uneducated
countries, where the soil is fertile, and where the
common comforts of animal life may be procured with
but little of bodily labour. Education, by quickening
and elevating the power of the mind, opens it to the
discovery of new wants; a people beginning to be
educated, are anxious to inform themselves of the state
and condition of other nations, with whom they hold
intercourse, and are gradually led to desire the refinements
and advantages of civilized life. There speedily follows,
as a natural consequence, a strong desire to improve the
construction of their dwelling-houses,—to procure better
furniture and better clothing,—to mend the roads and
highways,—to use horses instead of asses and mules
for purposes of draught and burden,—to improve the
construction of their rude and inconvenient carriages,
and to carry forward many other ameliorating measures.
An increase of labour will be immediately bestowed on
the soil, that the cultivators may be enabled to bring
greater quantities of produce to market, as by this
means only, can they hope to supply themselves with
the conveniences and luxuries which a new state of
society leads them to covet. Industry will thus succeed
to idleness, and both the natural face of the country,
and the manners and morals of the people, will undergo
a great change for the better.

Coincident with an extended school education, as
a means of regenerating Hayti, is the spread of the
Holy Scriptures in the French and Spanish languages,
and the diffusion of useful, moral, and religious treatises,

adapted to the minds of the young. The free toleration of all religious sects, which exists in the island, is highly favourable to efforts of this description; and such efforts, if conducted by exemplary individuals, who may settle in the country, or who may go to sojourn there for a time as visitors, would meet with ready support from many of the more enlightened inhabitants. An honest zeal in this department of labour, combined with the Christian example and Christian precept, of those who take part in it, would prove a great blessing. It would not be easy to estimate the advantages likely to result from the discriminating zeal of even a small body of Christian settlers, in a land like this. It was said by a religious reformer, two centuries ago, that a right-minded Christian, acting on all occasions as the Gospel prescribes, who should endeavour, in the spirit of his Lord and Master, to teach and enlighten others, would "shake the country for many miles round." Nor is this testimony, to the power of truth, an exaggeration. Let those who wish well to others, and who have ample pecuniary means at their disposal, encourage men and women of this stamp to enter on this field of labour,— persons, if such can be found, who are willing and qualified, and who feel urged by a sense of religious duty to undertake the mission. All are not required to leave their native homes, and to settle or travel in distant lands, where moral cultivation is at a low ebb; but all are bound, by the claims of Christian love, to look at moral destitution wherever it exists, and to use every means in their power, under the Divine blessing, to counteract or remove it. Exertions must be made to rescue the land from the degradation of intemperance,

which is one of its greatest evils; but we must look
to the progress of light and knowledge to effect this
object, rather than to any immediate measures on the
part of Temperance Societies. If education be encouraged
by the State, as there is reason to hope it will be;
if the Romish missals, and fabulous legends that now
constitute the principal reading of the few young people
who are taught in the schools, be dismissed from use,
and if works of history, of science, and of morals, be
substituted in their place, and the Holy Scriptures be
generally distributed and read, a new spirit would be
awakened in the minds of the rising generation, which
would gradually diffuse itself throughout the community; under its influence much moral evil would sub-
side, and sound views of what it is really the nation's
interest and duty to do, would speedily prevail. Temperance Societies might then work effectually, but will
be powerless for any extensive good, till this better
day shall dawn.

The corruptions of the priesthood, to which we have
so often adverted, are of too formidable a nature to be
easily overcome. If the priests were banished from the
island, could such a measure be justified, something as
bad as popery, or perhaps worse, would probably rise
to take its place; and nothing, for a long time at least,
would be gained to the cause of religion and morality,
by the exercise of a summary jurisdiction of this sort
against them. Much may be hoped for from the
extension of Protestant principles, and from their increasing influence; and to these, and to other causes,
operating religiously, we must look for a reformation
of character, both in priests and people, rather than

to the intervention of the civil magistrate. Some reformations, however, are needed, which are peculiarly within the province of a temporal government, and on which it would be wise for the government of Hayti immediately to enter, without waiting for time to develop those higher views of duty in the minds of the people, which must naturally flow from the diffusion and reception of religious truth. Improvements in prisons, and in prison-discipline, are of this sort; these might be effected speedily, at very little cost, and to great public advantage. A better code of criminal jurisprudence, and a wiser administration of it, are also urgently required; and the house of representatives, which feels the necessity of this change, instead of being rebuked by the executive for boldly stating its views, should be encouraged to persevere in its laudable course, for the public good. The standing army should be immediately cut down, not merely for the purpose just alluded to, of setting at liberty a fund to promote the cause of national education, although this is of paramount im- portance, but also to restore many thousands of able-bodied men to productive field-labour, who are now wasting their time on parade, and who, by their pilfering habits, and immoral manner of living, contribute, more than any other class, to the general demoralization. Let the army of Hayti be disbanded, and an active civil police force be organized in its stead; let the criminal jurisprudence of the land be reformed, together with its prisons and its prison discipline; let every encouragement be given to the extension of Protestant principles; above all, let a scheme of elementary education be devised, which shall be founded on Christian principles, unsectarian in its character, and so comprehensive as to embrace all the rising generation. Let these improvements be set on foot, and these reforms be administered, and then, as certainly as effect succeeds to cause, the republic of Hayti will be raised from the degradation under which it suffers; the moral and political face of the land will brighten; and the country, now pointed at by the proud finger of scorn as unworthy of notice, will assume her proper rank in the scale of nations, and compel the governments of Europe and America to yield her respect and honour.

JOHNSTON & BARRETT, Printers, 13, Mark Lane.

For EU product safety concerns, contact us at Calle de José Abascal, 56–1°,
28003 Madrid, Spain or eugpsr@cambridge.org.

www.ingramcontent.com/pod-product-compliance
Ingram Content Group UK Ltd.
Pitfield, Milton Keynes, MK11 3LW, UK
UKHW012342130625
459647UK00009B/485